ISLANDS

TOMMY RAYKOVICH

ISBN 979-8-88685-709-2 (paperback)
ISBN 979-8-88685-710-8 (digital)

Christian Faith Publishing, Inc.
832 Park Avenue
Meadville, PA 16335
www.christianfaithpublishing.com

Printed in the United States of America

1

The cool breeze blowing onshore felt refreshing to her face. She pulled the brim of her hat lower over her forehead to block the sun from her eyes. The warmth of it felt good on her arms. She'd ceased having any concern for the effects on her body. The tan shade of her skin complemented her auburn hair. She remembered how young women could spend significant sums each week at salons to achieve what she enjoyed. The absence of pale skin tone spoke of an active lifestyle to them. Seeking whatever advantage they could get, those young women tried to become what they were not. They desired the look she carried strolling on the beach. The sun's heat hadn't arrived. With its emergence, the pleasure in the light diminished.

The sand under her bare feet was a contentment she sought in the morning. It was the only time she could enjoy her walks without sandals. She could never remember walking without shoes as an adult. It just wasn't ladylike. She was still a woman. The lady faded after a few months on this island. She had a healthy, vibrant skin that glowed. Alexandria had always been a beautiful woman. This aided her in the men's world of finance. The men she worked with found it a pleasure to be in the same room with her. She was better than most of them; they never could find a reason to put her beneath themselves. In her presence, one couldn't help feeling a slight sense of awe.

Seeds of new life filled the coconut palm on her right. They'd only to drop and wash away with the outgoing tide. Somewhere, if it's destiny, one would land on a remote beach with the incoming tide. There, the cycle would begin again. She often wondered if someone on another island was gazing at a palm tree that was created from the one on her beach. It was these moments of reflection that opened the windows into her past life. She was thousands of miles from where the experiences occurred. She came this far to escape them. They seemed moments away. During the first few months after her arrival, her mind was still close to her past. She could never rid herself of it. After the first year, she embraced various memories. They were her companion on her morning walks. She had many good days back then. Yes, there were dark memories that she tried to keep pushed back out of her consciousness. She knew they'd always be there. She now had many activities to occupy her present. Her present now covered over her life story. She felt a sense of peace. It replaced the grief baggage she'd brought with her. She now stowed this baggage well away from her thoughts.

These walks brought back recollections of her days around Depoe Bay. She licked her lips. The sweet taste of the salt spray on them was a special flavor she'd enjoyed then. The sound of the surf coming from her side today was a familiar sound. Her senses now, as then, gave her the same message. Thoughts flowed over her as did the waves over the reef just offshore. She and Phillip had often discussed their relationship during that period, those times when they walked on the beach along the bay. It was a beach, not unlike the sand under her feet. She thought she was in love then, when she was young. Life was so gay, she remembered. The smell of the ocean was a perfume when they were sailing. Phillip had been her foundation after graduating from college. The events of life hadn't turned out as she'd planned.

Wonderful parents raised her. Her father was a smart business owner. He'd founded three successful companies. Being an only child, she was doted on by her father. He saw to her every need. A wise man with common sense raised her and always stopped short of spoiling her. It taught her that one had to work for what one wanted. He had. She saw it in his life and his work. It was a lesson that rewarded her well.

She'd sensed what she thought was love from her parents. But it wasn't the deep, heartfelt love that can happen in one's life. Her father focused on his businesses. He'd tried to make up for losing time with his daughter by replacing it with material things. He endeavored to make them his sign of love for her. Her mother followed the same pattern. She married a successful man. Her marriage allowed her to be the quintessential socialite, ever going from one event to another. She tried to show love during the brief moments when their lives occupied the same space and time. Alexandria had no complaints. She had her own life.

The woman was more akin to her father than her mother. She aspired for success because she saw what it gave her father, and she wanted that for herself. She wanted a degree in business, and it pleased her father. As a caring father, he paid the price for her to attend Stanford for that reason. He'd do his part, and he knew she'd do the rest. He'd shown her hard work, and it was worthwhile. She worked and studied hard. It was late spring in her senior year when her father called. He told her he and her mother wanted to see her before her graduation. They'd come in his private jet. She was looking forward to their visit. She and Phillip had been discussing marriage. Her parents had met and knew Phillip. They'd spoken to her of their approval not long after she'd met him in her junior year. He was attending Stanford as well. *How could father not approve?* she thought when she first introduced him. What happened later defied reasoning and logic. Those thoughts forever cast a dark shadow over her life. The plane crashed on approach; the reason remained a mystery. Someone attributed it to pilot error, as are most plane crashes. But the result was the same. Her parents were gone. Life as she knew it ceased. Another memory she longed to forget. It wasn't the only one.

Here, on this remote island, she escaped. She had run from many things. The clear green waters she saw were a far cry from the turbulent Pacific coast of Oregon. The theme on this island was serenity. It was soothing to the turbulence in her mind. She'd run far to escape that which she couldn't remove from her. First to Phillip, next to a world of greed and corruption. She dove into the latter. She bathed in it. It was far from the worlds she'd lost, and it washed the memories away. Then away again. Running again from experiences. *When will the tragedies cease? When can the running stop?* she asked herself. *Here on this volcanic rock in the heart of the Pacific Ocean*, she thought. What better place to stop fleeing from the torturing memories? There was nothing here. Nothing to remind her of those days she so longed to leave forgotten.

It's not as warm as it was yesterday, she reflected. Each morning on her beach distanced her from what she'd left. Each new day added to the distance. At present, it seemed, she couldn't see that far behind her. Now she only saw today, and it felt good. Her small, accommodating cabin was only a few yards over the dune. The grains of sand became her world. To many people, it would appear small. To Alexandria, it loomed large in her mind. The larger her world, the smaller her former life. She loved the coral reefs that was the ocean floor in her view. She preferred the scene from the beach rather than the cabin's deck.

This morning resembled most preceding mornings. The brown noddies were plentiful. She watched them swoop over the clear green water in search of food. The white terns were so abundant it was as if the sky over the island was filled with darting snowflakes. She scanned the beach in front of her for seashells. She always wanted to find a unique one to add to her collection. This collection was a hobby that she enjoyed. Looking at them in her cabin brought a sense of calm to her often troubled mind. She saw the simplistic beauty of their creation in the many shapes formed of calcium carbonate.

Peering along the shoreline, the figure of a large shell caught her attention. "Yes, yes," she cried out loud. She raced to the horned helmet shell at the water's edge. Picking it up, she caressed its form as a mother lovingly strokes the soft cheek of her child. She turned it in her hands, examining every feature of nature's art. "It's in perfect condition," she exclaimed. "This prize will add to my collection." In her excitement, she peered further up the beach. She expected to find something else special today.

A large object ahead caught her eye. *That wasn't there yesterday*, she thought. She walked toward it. Then she stopped. She realized this wasn't a piece of debris. The bright yellow life jacket was unmistakable. She dropped her prize and raced toward it. A man was lying on his stomach; the waves were flowing forward to touch his feet. His hands were tucked under his head—he was napping in the sun.

She knelt beside him. Putting her hand across the back of his neck, she felt the warmth of his body on her palm. Sliding her hand over to his shoulder, she gave it a gentle tug. "Hello," she said. "Can you hear me?" There was no response. Putting both hands around his opposite shoulder, she pulled him toward her, laying his head on her lap. The slightly blackened skin of his face showed he'd been very near to fire. The back of his hands showed the same feature. Years passed since she'd gazed into the face of a man close to hers. Instantly, Phillip's face replaced the face of the man in her arms. She tried to push the thought back. Forgotten emotions in her past flowed over her. The feelings of love and compassion that she'd locked away came forth. For a few seconds, it confused her. *Why am I feeling this?* She thought. *I don't know this person!*

She stroked his forehead and said again, "Can you hear me?"

A slight twitch of his head, an ever so faint movement of his eyelids, showed his awareness. She put her hand on one of his cheeks and stroked it. His eyes opened. She saw confusion in his expression. "It's okay. I think you're all right. Can you talk?"

A weak voice responded, "Where am I?"

"You're on Nu'ulopa. It's part of the islands of Samoa. Are you in pain? You're burned!"

"I think I'm okay," he said, his voice strained. He was aware of the pain of his burns again. "My face and hands hurt. I don't know how long I was in the water."

Alexandria saw a dazed look on his face. She needed to know if he had other injuries other than his burns. "Are you feeling pain anywhere else on your body?"

"I don't think so."

"Try to sit. I'll get behind you and help." Putting her hands behind his shoulders, she tried her best to push his upper body forward. With her effort, and with what little strength he could muster, he sat up. She put her arms around him to give support. "Do you think you can stand? Let me take off this life jacket. It's soaked and heavy." She untied the life jacket. Removing it, she tossed it aside. "We need to get you on your feet. Can you try?"

"If you help me. I think I can. I feel very weak."

He leaned his weight forward as she tightened her grip around his chest. "I'll help lift you up." With her help, he was on his feet.

"Just stand still for a moment. Let's be sure you can walk. My cabin's only a short distance away." She knew it'd be a journey for him, even with her help. *What if he can't walk to the cabin?* The thought crossed her mind. She knew she'd have to deal with it.

"I think I'm okay now. I'll try."

Putting one arm around his waist and holding his hand, she said, "Let's begin slowly. There's no one I can get to help."

He inched forward, like a newborn animal taking its first steps. Alexandria felt her authoritative instinct take control. "Do this. One foot in front of the other. I can't leave you here."

"I know. I'll do it. You could never carry me."

By their sheer will and her determination, they made it to the steps leading to her cabin. The few looked daunting to them.

"Sit on the bottom step and rest," she instructed him. "I'll get a glass of water." She looked at him as she helped him sit. She could tell he was near exhaustion. Perceived compassion came over her again. *Why am I experiencing this?* she thought. There was a problem, and she was dealing with it. She had dealt with problems all her life. She always dealt with them emotionless. A problem only needed to be solved. She'd never had time to *feel* anything about problems. All these years on this island, had she suppressed the emotions of her life? Had she tried to bury her past so deep that she had buried her emotions with it? Memories are the moments of life we bring along on the journey. The emotions evoked by the experiences are the proper rewards of the journey. Alexandria, losing what she didn't want, had discarded what made life worthwhile. She didn't understand this concept. But it was becoming a lesson now. Hurrying up the steps, she knew she had to get him in the house. His last ounce of strength would leave him soon. She returned with a glass of water.

"Drink this. You appear dehydrated." She put the glass to his lips. Turning the glass upward, he eagerly drank the cool liquid.

"Thank you."

"You've little strength left. You must get up the steps. I can take care of you in the house. You can't stay here."

"I know. Shove me there if necessary."

With great effort from both, they reached the open door. He almost fell.

"Just a few steps to the couch. It's close."

Reaching for it, he collapsed onto the cushions. She put a throw pillow under his head. Grabbing his feet, she swung them around, putting them on the couch. His eyes closed, and he drifted into unconsciousness.

Taking a deep breath, she stood and looked at this stranger in her house. *An hour ago, I was alone in my world. Now I've a man in my life*, she realized. A man! In a valley devoid of thought, a dam had burst. It had released a torrent of memories held behind its wall, and it overwhelmed her. She saw Phillip on her couch. She was with him again.

2

After her parents died, Phillip became her life. It was as he told her it'd be. He was there for her, and he wouldn't leave her. He saw she completed her finals and graduated. She never knew how she did it. It was because of Phillip's love and devotion. Moving past that terrible day was because of him. That day she learned of the crash. It haunted her for years. Phillip in her life blocked out that memory. A vibrant present diminishes a past one longs to forget. She told Phillip she wanted to continue her education and get a master's in business administration degree. She wanted it for herself and to honor her father. Phillip agreed. She did just that. Those years with Phillip were beyond anything she'd dreamed.

The woman dreamed. Dreaming was frequently in her mind. His presence was there as well. She first considered him when she awoke each morning. She last reflected on him before sleeping. There were times her subconscious took over. Alexandria controlled the external part of her life. She never understood how she could lose control of the internal. Her entire life was this way. Long ago, she concluded it was because she grew up as an only child. Having the usual casual friends didn't help. She'd never been close to any of them. She would never have told them her thoughts. So she and her thoughts grew up together. They were her life's companion. The two never parted. They created the illusions and dreams that sometimes seemed to define her existence. They had become a reality within her. The inward thinking happened more often now than it used to. She tried to control it, to prevent it. Never having been able, she accepted it.

She dreams more…then the man on her couch moaned.

She snapped back to where she stood. Dreaming about this man on her couch wasn't a choice. He wouldn't turn into someone else. Alexandria had many shortcomings, but she'd had a considerate heart at one time in her life. Her career at work had hardened it. A glimmer of that kindness flashed. Emotions hidden in the dark crevices of her mind returned to her life. This poor soul was hurting. Throwing him back into the water wasn't an option. In her flight from her past, she'd run from men. She'd been reclusive since arriving in Samoa. Enjoying an occasional visit to Apia, the capital, she avoided being friendly around men she encountered, lest they think otherwise. But she knew she couldn't avoid this man in her house. *I'll have to tend to him*, she thought.

Her cabin was a traditional Samoan *fale*. In addition to the interior latticework walls, she added a few solid walls she was accustomed to. But she liked the aesthetics of the native housing. Being above the beach, it caught the full effect of the trade winds. This was one benefit of the tropical islands, natural air-conditioning. A breeze cooled the open interior even on warm days. It was always comfortable unless you lay in wet clothes. She knew he'd get chilled in his wet clothes. She went to her bedroom. Returning with a blanket, she placed it over him. She sat in the chair beside the couch. Her mind was spinning with anamneses triggered by this event. Realizing the effort of their trip from the beach had tired her, she closed her eyes and fell asleep.

When she opened her eyes, he was still asleep. Maybe an hour had passed. He needed to sleep longer. She knew she'd have to take care of him for the short term. She surmised his injuries were superficial, and his major problem was dehydration. With food and rest, she knew his strength would return. This was an uninhabited island, and her friend Iosefa had brought her supplies only yesterday. He wouldn't return for another week. It didn't pose a problem to her. She always kept more than enough supplies and food for an extended period. They'd provide the unexpected houseguest with what he needed.

Alexandria was a resourceful woman. She knew how to live and survive on a remote island. It was the life she had chosen. Here, she did as she pleased. The rules of society didn't constrain her. Nor did she have to cope with society. The callous and self-serving approach to people bothered her. Each had their own values, always in conflict with the others. This she'd left behind. It didn't haunt her as other memories. Losing this pleased her.

She could handle any emergency, even a man "washing up" on her beach. The medical supplies were available, and the food would be adequate. An ocean of protein existed to sustain her and him. She realized she didn't have clothing for a man. She'd find a solution. Problem-solving was her best trait. Her career had been that until she gave it up to come here. This man needed help to get his strength back. She wondered, *How could he wash up on my beach in the Pacific Ocean? And who is he?*

Going into another room, she returned with medical supplies, towels, and a robe. She prepared to make a pot of coffee and a meal. As she began, a mild feeling of pleasure came over her. She didn't cook for someone other than herself. Iosefa's visits were brief when he brought her supplies. It was a short boat ride from the main islands. He never stayed long. Longing for conversation, she'd occasionally ask him to stay for a while. She always prepared something for him to eat during those visits. He was full-blood, native Samoan and had not the taste for Western food culture. He always ate out of respect for his friend. They'd formed a simple friendship. Upon her arrival at Samoa, the contractor she'd hired to build her cabin had introduced her to him. Iosefa had a boat he used for fishing charters. America's scent was still fresh in her nostrils. That which she'd run from was vivid in her mind. She didn't want a boat. It'd mean she'd make frequent trips to the main island for supplies. It was civilization, the same as she had escaped. She wanted no part of it nor the memories it invoked. Iosefa and she had made an agreement to bring her supplies. She paid him more than he could make on a fishing charter, and it was regular pay. It was a mutually beneficial arrangement.

The stranger in her cabin stirred something deep inside of her. She enjoyed cooking a meal for two, but there was something else. She didn't know what it was and didn't dwell on it. The fragrance of an emotion was wafting in her mind's sense of smell. It created a similar sense as spices heating in a sauté pan does to the nostrils; the senses are aware of them. Alexandria's want to mute her past had in effect dulled her senses. She'd induced on herself a sensory deprivation state the last three years. She'd no idea how it had affected her. Evil wasn't part of her personality. She'd known happiness and sadness, pleasure and pain, joy and sorrow. At one time in her life, she'd experienced the full range of human emotions. She'd thought emotions were born out of the events in one's life, and the temporal happenings of her days created the reality perceptions that made up life. She'd forgotten it was the emotions inspired by those happenings that make the genuine gifts of life. When she dug the grave to bury her past, she wasn't aware how much she'd placed in the coffin with it. With the sadness, she had placed her happiness. With her pain, she had placed her pleasure. Added with her losses were her gains. She'd created a new world on this island. It was a world without memories. At least she tried for it to be. And the harder she tried, the deeper she buried her emotions. She still had a few that gave her pleasure each day. But a solitary environment placed a small limit on them. One cannot cut out emotions one doesn't want like cancer and extradite them. They're placed in us at our creation. They never leave us even if we try to leave them. Alexandria was reexperiencing what would always be a part of her. It was subtle to her mind. She was becoming aware of it.

With the fresh supplies, she had an assortment of vegetables. She always prepared them in the days soon after Iosefa's visit. Having only the minimal equipment needed, she couldn't store them long. With a cut of beef and the vegetables, she prepared a hearty soup. It's what this man needed. She'd enjoy the uncommon treat as well. She wasn't aware of the smile on her face as she prepared and cooked the soup. As the soup simmered, she set the table. The smell in the kitchen mixing with the fresh sea air created a fragrance that brought back a memory of another smell. It is said the sense of smell is the most powerful trigger to memory recall.

Suddenly, she was in a new spring grass meadow covered with assorted wildflowers. She and Phillip were hand in hand. The aroma of the petals filled her nostrils. It had engraved their essence in her mind. Their eyes were always looking at the other. *I hope this bliss will never end*, she said with glee in her voice.

She shook her head. *Where did that thought come from?"* she wondered. She refocused on what she was doing, preparing a pot of coffee. In a short while, she heard him stirring.

Going to the couch, she saw his eyes were open. "How are you feeling?" she asked.

"Like I washed up on a beach," he answered with a faint grin.

"I've medical supplies. I'll tend to your burns. Would you like a cup of coffee?"

"Yes," he said, smiling this time.

She poured a cup of coffee and set it on the table beside the couch. "Can you sit up?" He labored at this simple task but did it. He took the cup of coffee and eagerly swallowed a sip.

"That tastes wonderful."

"I've prepared a pot of soup. I'll tend to your burns first. They don't appear too severe. Salt water has an amazing healing and therapeutic effect on wounds. I'll put ointment on them. It should ease the pain. I think it's best to leave them open to the air for healing. The skin doesn't appear blistered or broken."

"Thank you. You're very kind."

"I don't get guests who just drop in. Just trying to be a wonderful hostess." When she made that statement, she was aware again of that strange sensation she didn't understand. It felt good to her. Conversation was a part of her personality. Alexandria's extrovert character made her comfortable with other people. That was a huge part of her success. She made others feel at ease with her. She could engage anyone in discourse. There was a wit to her dialogue everyone enjoyed. This latent ability was reemerging. She finished caring for his burns.

"Would you like a bowl of soup?"

"Very much."

"Can you make it to the table?"

"Yes. I'm feeling much better after my rest."

She assisted him from the couch and into a chair at the table. Going to the stove, she returned with a bowl of soup. Placing it in front of him, she went back and brought herself a bowl of soup. She sat on the opposite side of the table.

"What's your name?" she asked.

A puzzled looked came over him. He blinked his eyes. His lips moved, as if trying to speak. "I…I don't remember!" The spoon fell from his hand into the soup.

"It's okay," she said. "You've had an unpleasant experience. Don't worry about it now. Eat your soup."

He picked up the spoon and did as she told him. His mind was in a fog. "I don't remember my name!"

"We'll discuss that later. Right now, the priority is getting your strength back. Now, relax and eat." He was hungry and did. When he'd eaten his meal, he wanted to go back to the couch. She helped him there and sat beside him.

"Let's take it slow. You don't remember your name. What do you remember? You must've been on a boat. Were other people on the boat? Where did you come from? There was a fire. What can you remember?"

"I remember a boat. It wasn't a large boat, not a cruise ship. Maybe it was a small boat, like a cabin cruiser. I don't remember if there were other people. I remember being on a boat and leaving an island. There was a fire. Pictures just flash in my mind."

"I'm not a medical expert, but I know it's common after a traumatic event. You need to rest and regain your strength. I'm sure by tomorrow you'll be feeling better."

"I hope you're right. Help clear my confusion. Who are you, and where am I?"

"My name is Alexandria Denton. My friends call me Alex. I don't have many here. Please call me Alex. You're on an isolated island of Samoa." Another sensation came over her. Feeling a compulsion to say more than the answer to his questions, she continued. "This is where I wanted to live. I escaped the world I knew. Many people want to escape from their world. Jobs, marriages, money—many things trap them. Reflecting on the years, they ask themselves, 'Did you ever think life would turn out like this?' Many can't leave their present. Many can't leave their past. We each have that which holds us. It may be good, and it may not be good. We make our priorities in life, and then we must live with them unless something takes them from us. I had the resources, and more than that, I'd the desire to escape. What I escaped from is my business. So I left and came here. I love it. The isolation and I've become pleasant companions. The poet John Donne wrote, 'No man is an island entire of itself; every man is a part of a continent, a part of the main.' Well, I'm not a man, so I don't think that philosophy applies to me. I enjoy being an *island* on an island. It suits me just fine."

It intrigued him. He wanted to know more. "You said 'the world that you knew.' It was a well-to-do world to afford to come here, well-tended. You left a lot to come here. Why leave so much for so little?"

"You ask many questions, whoever you are. Especially for someone that can't remember anything, not even his name. I'd think you'd want to find out about yourself, not me!"

3

The statement caught him off guard. "I'm sorry. Something wrapped me up in your story. Everything's so puzzling now. My mind's spinning. I'd feel better out of these wet clothes. I can't think now."

"Here's a towel and a robe. I'll leave the room for a few minutes. I married once. We're divorced now. We'll be in close quarters for a while. Don't be embarrassed. I'll wash and dry your clothes. The cabin has off-the-grid facilities. I left my old world, not all my comforts." She left the room.

As she entered her bedroom, the burst dam continued to pour out its contents of memories she thought she had purged from her consciousness. Her thoughts were spinning the same as his. She lay on the bed as her mind swirled with long suppressed reminders of her days with Phillip. Phillip! He was a lifeboat to her after her parents died. Oh, how she thought she loved him then. Never having experienced genuine love, her relationship with him was a learning expedition. But she never doubted his love for her. It showed in his devotion and benevolent consideration toward her. She tried to emulate his behavior. In her vulnerability the first few months after her parents died, she identified with Phillip. Not knowing how to show love, she mimicked his actions toward her. The girl had learned one side of love growing up with her parents. She knew how to receive love; they did not show her how to give genuine love. Her parents found it more convenient, and less time-consuming, to show love with objects. They never gave the most valuable gift, the gift of time. Everyone has this limited resource. If diverted from other things and directed at one special person, it flows from one spring. The source of its intention is love. One will only give their most valuable possession out of love. From this outpouring, nothing is held back. An intimacy grows. This wasn't the case with Alex. She'd stopped short of this.

Being strong-willed and independent, she recognized her vulnerability with her relationship with Phillip when she needed him. In giving herself over to his care, she guarded this part of her being. She needed his help but didn't want to relinquish complete control to him. Her love for him grew out of commitment and passion. With commitment, she saw a future together. With passion, she felt a strong affection, devotion, and fondness for Phillip. She characterized these as love. But she lacked the third ingredient of genuine agape love, intimacy with Phillip. This intimacy differs from a physical one. Alex couldn't come to reveal her true nature to him. Not that she had anything to hide. She was an extrovert and an introvert. She was gregarious and unreserved for those around her. But she turned inward concerning her emotional and spiritual being. She held these parts of her close, not to be shared with anyone, even Phillip. Unaware of doing so, it had by then become part of her character. One cannot make biscuits without leavening. One cannot experience love without all the ingredients. Without revealing one's innermost thoughts to the other, one can never be intimate with one's mate. So that person could never be completely in love. This was a lesson Alex hadn't understood.

When she returned to the university, she'd focused most of her time and energy on obtaining her post-graduate degree. She hadn't given Phillip the time she should have. He bowed to her wishes. She completed her studies and graduated near the top of her class. A large privately held investment firm offered her a prominent starting position. Before she started, he took her on a sailing trip along the coast. Phillip loved sailing almost as much as he loved her. It was along the Oregon coast that her life changed dramatically again. She'd distracted him with her caress. He could never refuse her advances.

He stopped focusing on the nearby rocks in the rough waters. The haunting sound of the boat slamming against the rocks would never leave her. The damage was complete, and the event threw Phillip overboard. She put on a life vest and dove in after him. She never saw him again. It cost them both dearly. To Alex, when Phillip died, she'd lost her lover. In one respect, she had. In her life, the definition wouldn't have meant anything to her. He was gone, and it was real. The grief she felt was real. It was more pronounced than when her parents died. But the worst part was she felt that she'd caused his death. She ran from it to her new job. There she was Alexandria Denton, a new employee with no yesterday.

She returned to the primary room. He had changed. His clothes were in a damp heap on the floor. Reaching down, she gathered the heap in her arms. "I'll care for these. Pour yourself another cup of coffee. I'm self-sufficient here. You'll have to learn the same. I'll help you, not pamper you." She turned and left the room.

He was in the presence of a determined and self-reliant person.

No wonder she's well off, he thought. *Whatever she did, I know she was a success at it.* Mixed emotions filled his thoughts. He hadn't explained the complete reason for how he came to be on her beach this morning. This troubled him. But he was in competent hands and okay, for now. It could've ended much worse. He also realized his devious ways wouldn't work with her. All his charm wouldn't get past her defenses. He knew this was a special woman. *I'm glad I'm feeling better,* he thought. *She may want me to go out and catch my dinner.*

Alex returned to the room carrying a different bundle. "These'll do for now," she said. "I've a pair of overalls and a couple pair of T-shirts and a few shorts. I know you don't want to spend your time here in my robe. If a neighbor came to borrow a cup of sugar, what would they think of you? Your clothes are still okay. I'll have them washed and dried in a few hours. Then you'll have a complete wardrobe." The levity felt good to her. This trait had served her well with clients. She always put them at ease. Of the many tools in her tool belt, it was her Judas goat. She used it to lure her prey into her pen. There, when she cornered them, they knew they'd met their match. Cunning was one of many ways her fellow employees described her.

His strength had returned to him, and so had his faculties. "You're one of the calmest people I've ever met. You act like you handle this situation every week," he said with admiration.

"Trust me. This isn't an experience I'm proficient in. Dealing with problems is. I see a challenge and know I can handle it. I can handle you. But now, I want more information. Please sit. We need to talk." Alex had left her past life. Leaving the memories associated with that life, she wanted a new start and a new life. She'd found it on this remote speck in the Pacific Ocean. What she couldn't leave behind was who she was. Alex was always in command. She seldom asked permission. She charged ahead; damn the torpedoes. It brought her success and recognition from the gray hairs on the top floor. It was who she was, and she hadn't left it. She hadn't been who she was since arriving on her island. She had the chance now. It created contentment.

He knew he couldn't question or debate this woman. He sat up straight on the couch as he spoke. "I should thank you for what you've done for me. I'd be dead now if you hadn't found me on the beach. But beyond that, the care you've given me is over what one could expect. I only want to say thank you." He didn't know how much weight it'd carry, but at least he'd show gratitude. He hoped it'd win him a few points.

"You're welcome," she replied. "That's who I am." She had a serious look on her face. She was back in her environment. It could've been another mega-million-dollar deal involving a large corporation. It may have been a small acquisition with great potential returns in the future. Or it could be the interrogation of a stranger on her couch. She approached them the same. She began. "You couldn't have been in the water more than a day or the sharks would've had you. I saw your burns, so something bad happened. From what you've told me so far, I surmise you were on a fair-sized boat. No one takes off over the open waters of the Pacific in a canoe. You were going somewhere alone. I don't think the event, whatever it was, would've caused you to forget someone with you. Something happened on that boat. It was a fire you couldn't control. You ended up in the water and on my beach. I don't see that so traumatic to cause temporary amnesia. I think you need to level with me."

Damn! She's good! he thought to himself. His mind raced. He needed a plausible answer. She wouldn't buy into any more of his fantasies. *I'll have to tell the truth. Well, maybe a little.*

"Okay, okay," he answered. "Here's the truth. You left to escape something. I know it was a well-paid job. But you left to escape something else. I can tell. I won't ask you what. People don't leave what they love. You've something to tell as well. But I'll answer your question. I left to escape something. It involved me in what's referred to as white-collar crime. Working as a financial advisor in a large firm, I saw a way to get ahead. I skimmed. I left to flee from the authorities. Are you shocked?" He paused, waiting for an answer.

"No," she replied. "I know it happens." She sat back and waited.

"I did it over a few years. It added up fast. I put the proceeds into shell accounts. A few days ago, I took it out in negotiable bearer bonds. I bought a fair-sized boat and was going to island-hop to Samoa. Next, a plane to nowhere, nowhere anyone would find me. Then, a leak in a fuel line. A fire, and guess what, my bearer bonds are at the floor of the Pacific Ocean. You can turn me in if you want. But I must warn you. There'll be no reward. I thought I could bluff my way with a wonderful story. Realizing it won't work with you, I confess. Okay, now what?"

"Fascinating story. Would you like another bowl of soup? Or can I fix you something better?" she replied, unfazed. Past negotiations with her adversaries came into her mind. She loved those times. Alex knew this love. This love made her feel good. This was her love then. She'd replaced one love with another. To Alex, the latter had become as satisfying as her first. She felt her pulse quicken when she'd enter a boardroom to discuss her terms with the members of the board of the corporation she was going to acquire. She knew she was. They didn't at that moment. She could read the uncertainty in their eyes. She'd take control. After the meeting, members of the board would leave with the same thought. *What just happened?* This man's life now was another puzzle to be solved. She knew she'd win again.

"What do you have?" he inquired, astounded at her question.

"I caught two grouper yesterday. I can prepare them. Iosefa brought a few potatoes. I've some chardonnay I've been saving. I think it'd pair well with the fish. What do you think?" she asked.

"It beats what I had yesterday. Do we need to make reservations?"

"No, I own the place. Relax. I haven't cooked a proper meal for someone in a long time. Do you *remember* how to open a bottle of wine?" she said, looking into his face.

Understanding her emphasis, he replied, "Yes. My memory returned. There are many things that I remember. I remember intelligent women. Now I'm with one. Where's the wine?"

"It's in the wine cabinet. Bottom left. The pots and bowls are there. I make do with what I have."

"The wine glasses are…the first two glasses I find. Is that correct?"

"Yes. You're catching on fast."

"Yes, I am."

They were both at ease. The conversation was refreshing to them for many reasons. It had been a long time since they had enjoyed a moment such as this.

Alex finished preparing the meal, and they sat at the table to enjoy their feast. Alex felt emotions coming from her mind as the tulips emerge from a long winter of isolation. Her years of isolation had been a hibernation of her spirit. She'd never concluded this point. She was aware of suppressing what she didn't want to face again. Her soul now thirsted for the water of the spirit. Without human contact, the soul withers and dies. This contact had always been a large part of Alex's life. She was only now realizing how much she needed it.

"This is the best fish I've ever eaten," he said sincerely.

"Thank you," she said, smiling. "I'm glad you're appreciating your meal. I've always found delight in cooking. It's been a long time since I've cooked for a man other than Iosefa. But I'll not cook for a *nameless* man again!"

Her point didn't need clarification. He understood. He knew his hostess was a strong, determined woman. She'd saved his life and was now providing everything he needed. He had faults, but ingratitude wasn't one of them.

"My name is Geoffrey Scott. I worked for World Resource Security Investments in Australia. I've worked for various firms over the years. That's just the last one. I learned plenty and stole much. I'm guilty of that. Do I get kicked off the island?"

"No, you can stay for now. Just don't get too comfortable. I still don't know you. I only know what you've told me. You've told me you're not a credible person. We're here together. Just remember, you've got permission for nothing! If you don't approve of the accommodations, your lifejacket is still on the beach. If you doubt I can take care of myself, I can remove that doubt. Let's finish our meal and wine. I waste nothing here." Thus, they did. It was a relatively pleasurable experience for both, all things considered.

Geoffrey felt admiration for his dinner companion. He had never known a woman of such character. He could sense her commanding nature. She wasn't a General Patton. But the precept of her presence in a room would be for respect. Alex's feelings were nothing like Geoffrey's. Hers followed a more feminine attribute. Her character didn't eliminate the essence of her sex. It absorbed her with thoughts of her dinner companion. She couldn't understand why. There was a mystery to him. She knew there was more to his story than he'd told. But she knew what she liked about him. He'd been as ruthless in his job as she was with hers. She saw common ground in their jobs. The past, long packed away, was now part of her daily life. She couldn't avoid it.

When they had finished their meal, Alex rose from her chair. "I'm going to bed," she stated. "Your bed is the couch. If you need anything, deal without it. I'll see you in the morning. You can do the dishes then." She turned and left the room.

Of all the beaches to wash up on…! he thought. *Well, at least I'm safe and well fed. My story didn't seem to bother her. And we're alone. A good night's sleep will make me feel better. I need my wits about me with her. I know she's not telling me everything about herself either.* He lay on the couch and was asleep.

Alex had excused herself early. She needed to think. So much was stirring in her. People, places, events of her life stored away churned in her consciousness. Faces flashed like a slideshow. She couldn't stop it. *Why had this Geoffrey person caused this?* she wondered. *Was it him, or was it me? I'd run as far as I could. Why can't I forget what I don't want to remember?* She was coming to a new rationalization. Her past wasn't an event in a specific place she could destroy by forgetting. One can destroy a photograph, but one cannot destroy the emotions created at the time of that picture. The emotion of love will stay even if the object of that love is gone. Alex's control couldn't control her mind. This clarity she understood. She lay in bed thinking, eventually drifting off to a fragmented sleep.

4

Geoffrey awoke to the smell of coffee brewing and bacon cooking. *Bacon*, he thought. *I must be dreaming.* Looking up, he saw Alex in the kitchen. "How did you get to the market and back so quickly?" he asked.

"Iosefa brings me a specific list of foods I want every time he comes. He always includes a few special things each visit. He enjoys surprising me. This trip he brought me a package of bacon. It's a rare treat. I thought you'd enjoy it as well. I hope you slept okay on the couch. I never planned this house for overnight guests. If people keep washing up on my beach, I may have to add on an extra room. You're wondering about the facilities here. I equipped the house with solar panels out back. They supply enough power for my basic needs, a small refrigerator, and a few lights. The stove runs on propane. I've a rainwater harvesting system that supplies me with fresh water. It's low now. I have to conserve it for drinking until it rains. If you want a bath, use the tub on the beach. I've other necessities. I'll explain more later. He also brought fresh eggs. I'll share them with you. Help yourself to the coffee."

She appears to be in a good mood this morning, he thought. *I need to take it slow. I can assume nothing about her. We're going to be here a while.*

"Thanks again for everything you did for me yesterday. I feel almost normal today. Whatever you put on my burns helped. I barely notice any pain today." He looked at her with an appreciative smile.

"That's okay. Come and sit at the table. Let's eat while the food is hot."

They enjoyed their meal, neither saying much. Alex couldn't help glancing up from her plate to look at this stranger in her house. She was trying to assess him. She knew she knew nothing about him. He wasn't truthful with her. She'd didn't know if he would be. Understanding what was going on in people's minds was a gift. This was how she'd made her living, and a good living it was. She deduced what her counterparts wanted. They never knew what to expect from her. She always kept her prey guessing, never knowing.

Alex and Geoffrey savored the flavors and tastes of this simple meal. They also, though not admitting it, enjoyed being in the company of the other. It was a special breakfast though both were unaware why. Still subtle, a strange relationship was forming. It was out of the cognizance of their thoughts. It was real nonetheless. On the surface, it would've appeared to be adversarial. In one sense, it was. But the effect of their facile relationship was developing. Neither grasped the occurrence. Each felt captivated by the other.

After they'd finished, Alex said, "Let's have another cup of coffee on the porch. The breeze is refreshing there." Refilling their cups, they went to the porch. "Geoffrey, I've been thinking," she stated. "I know you aren't telling me the entire story. But you didn't deliberately burn yourself, put on a life jacket, jump into shark-infested waters, and swim to my island. So I believe the story of a fire on the boat. But you're a smart man. I can tell this. You're also a liar and a cheat. You have these traits to do what you did. I think you were good at it. You tried it on me, but I know those tricks. But there's a flaw in your story. A smart con man wouldn't put all his eggs in one basket, especially not a briefcase full of bearer bonds. Your ill-gotten gains aren't at the bottom of the Pacific Ocean. They're in numbered accounts in the Cayman Islands. That's the *nowhere* you were going. You have a phony passport and ID in safekeeping. You'd take out your money once there and set up phony paper corporations in

Russia, Singapore, maybe Mali. Then you'd disperse the funds. The money trail would soon disappear, and you'd live happily ever after. Did I miss anything?"

Geoffrey shook his head. *I was right about this woman*, he thought. *One smart cookie!*

"No," he answered. "And you're not a farm girl from Nebraska either. You know about finance. That's how you made your money. You got what you have here with your resources. You know my story now. I'd like to hear yours."

Alex felt she was back in a boardroom, and she had won another battle. She felt she'd made him tell her the truth. Now a strange perception came over her. In the past, she would've walked out a victor, never revealing her motives or methods. Since this man washed up on her beach, her perception of reality continued to change. She was no longer living in the present, afraid of her past. She longed for, no, needed to speak of things forgotten. Alex was understanding. Forgotten, never to be brought to mind, were words sung on New Year's Eve. They could never be a conscious act on her part. She'd answer his question. Not because he wanted an answer. She'd answer it because she wanted to.

"I don't think I've anything on my social calendar today. I may as well. Yes, I was in finance. I was high in a large investment firm in the States. I married an attorney who worked for the same firm. I was in corporate acquisitions. With my guidance, it was a very profitable part of the firm. I was good at picking the right company to buy at the right time. I'd find a company going through a rough business cycle. We'd make the stockholders and the executive staff an offer they couldn't refuse. You know what I'm talking about. I'm sure you had contacts. You made your clients, and yourself, a lot of money buying and selling stocks on this information. Everyone in your business did it. You were likely more flagrant at it than others." She paused, looking at him.

He looked at her and nodded his head.

She continued. "Once we owned a controlling interest in the company, we'd carve it up, sell off the assets, and everyone went home happy and wealthier. Many employees, however, were out of work.

I turned a blind eye to that. The firm was making money from my work as fast as we could reinvest it. I received my fair share. I played the game, the same as you. Unlike you, I did it legally.

"One day I'd prepared a tender offer for a mid-sized manufacturing firm. The grandson of the founder ran it. With the stock in many hands, he lacked a controlling interest. We made the offer at the annual stockholders' meeting. He knew they'd sell. The man also knew what we'd planned. He came to see me. He begged me to forgo the deal. I pointed out to him how much money he'd receive. He said he didn't care about the money. It was a family business. I was disinterested in his concerns. He left my office, dejected. The weeks went by, and we completed the acquisition. I was preparing the plans to resell the company in pieces when my secretary came into my office. She'd printed a newspaper article from the town the company I just spoke of is located. She showed me the article. The grandson of the founder of the company I mentioned had put a gun to his head and killed himself."

Alex stopped talking. Geoffrey knew she needed to compose herself. He realized something emotional had happened to her in that moment. Silently, he waited.

Alex took a deep breath and began again. "I couldn't forget the look on his face as he left my office that day. When I got home that evening, I told my husband what I told you." He was unfazed. He told me, 'Forget about it. These things happen in business.' It was at that moment I realized the business I was in. I was in the business of ruining people's lives for a profit. I packed a suitcase and left. My husband and I were never in love. It was a marriage of convenience. I called him a couple of days later. I told him I wanted a divorce. If he didn't make trouble, I'd accept a reasonable amount. He could keep the rest. Our investments were massive. He agreed. And now, I'm here."

"I was right," Geoffrey said. "We're both running from our pasts." They both sat looking over the vast expanse of water, neither saying a word.

5

Alex spoke first. "Yes, Geoffrey, I ran away. I ran to get far away from the life I'd lived. I didn't want to read about people doing what I'd been doing. I didn't want to hear of people losing jobs. I'd known the greed of wanting more money than I could ever spend. I ran away from my guilt. Here, on my island, it was only a memory that had faded. Then you arrived. I feel the remorse I ran away from returning. I wish the current had taken you somewhere else."

The sensitivity of this subject bit into her like a savage animal. She had spent years suppressing her guilt. It was now a torrent of self-judgment condemning her again. She wrote the last three years on a blackboard. This man erased it. She now had no present, only her past. It was like her first day on this island. She'd have to start over again.

"Geoffrey, you don't understand. I've been running most of my life. I had nothing when I was young. I lived with wealthy parents. We had money. I know now we had little else. As I was growing up, the purpose of life was getting more money. I loved money, and I once thought I loved a man. I lost the love of both. That's when I came here. Here, I thought I'd found something to love. I loved losing the memories of my life. Now you've taken that love from me. I'm tired of losing what I love!"

Geoffrey knew this was a different Alex talking from the one he'd been listening to. The strong-willed, dominant personality she'd

27

shown wasn't here at this moment. He saw a woman speaking with emotion. He knew he'd have to talk to her now, on her level. She was revealing her innermost thoughts to him, a stranger. He could sense the intimacy growing between them. Lying to her had no benefit. He viewed any earlier relationships in life as how he could gain from them. A strange perception came over him. He now sought nothing to gain. It was as if he felt compelled to respond in kind. This was new to him. His brain had disengaged; he felt only what was in his heart. It occurred to him he'd never considered that he had two hearts. One was physical; the other he'd just discovered even existed in him. This woman told of her private life as if he was a close family member. Here she was, telling about it to an outsider.

"Alex, I know how you feel in one respect. I saw the corporate takeovers you described. When I saw the opportunity, I made money with the same fervor as you did. But I was far removed. I never thought of it as you described. I wasn't dealing with people. I was dealing with numbers on a computer screen. I was making money for other people. So much that they never questioned me. When you tell a client, 'I made you a hundred thousand dollars on a trade this week,' they're thrilled. That it was a hundred and twenty thousand wasn't necessary. Everyone was pleased. I looked at it as you did. It was a job, and I played the game. I don't want to sound cold and unfeeling. You have feelings. I do too. You've faced yours. I haven't faced mine. Maybe it's time I did." He looked at her to gauge her reaction.

"I've been here three years, Geoffrey. It's been a long time. You brought my past up. Now I'll put it away again. I worked with people like you. They were business colleagues. We were doing the same thing. Everyone's life was the pursuit of money. In reflection, I don't recall anyone discussing family or friends. We'd all refined the aspects of love into only two. The only loves seen at work were money and self. What a sad state I was in! No one spoke honestly. An accepted practice was getting ahead in the firm at the expense of a coworker. We're being honest with each other. I find it refreshing to talk to someone as ruthless as I was. I feel we are on a different level from what I experienced then. We've a lot in common. I want to hear more about you. Geoffrey, you must be honest with me. I've had enough lies in my life. I want to hear no more."

"Thank you, Alex. I've no fear of revealing anything to you. I'm not a compulsive liar. I did it as a tool of my trade. My weapon was to convince my clients I'd their best interests in mind. I was good at it. They believed my lies. I've nothing to gain from lying to you. Besides, I am indebted to you, as I should be. You saved my life. Maybe one of my few redeeming characteristics is gratitude. I owe you more than the truth."

"Yes, you do. Since you'll be here for a while, we may at least be friends. But don't lie to me anymore, Geoffrey," she stated bluntly.

"I won't. I'll make a genuine statement now. I like you," he said with a smile on his face.

"You've not spoken of any redeeming qualities about your life before arriving here. But I may like you too. Let's go for a walk on the beach," she said, returning the smile.

The weariness Geoffrey had felt was only an awareness now. Alex's statements had stirred retrospections up from the bottom of the bucket where he had tossed them. He thought of his childhood. It was so different from how Alex had described hers. But he could identify parts of his family life with hers. Their childhoods were similar and different. His father worked long hours but at middle-class jobs. He worked hard because he needed money. His mother worked also but for meager pay. They spent little of their spare time with him or his sister. They'd exposed him to love. He saw it in his parents' relationship. They needed each other. They'd formed their own version of a love relationship. But the love wasn't from their hearts. It was from companionship on a common journey. They'd attended to the needs of him and his sister. He saw it now as a duty they felt obligated to do. To them, it was their love for their children. Their love was a sense of responsibility, nothing more. Geoffrey's parents showed love by an appearance like Alex's. But to neither of them was it truly given. Their parents didn't expose genuine love to their children. Alex and Geoffrey had the same association with love. It was something one received. Neither had children as an adult. So the commitment to give love, as they thought it, didn't exist in their worlds.

Geoffrey knew Alex had taken him into her confidence. *Take it slow*, he thought to himself. *I need her to want to help me. I've better places to be.*

"I'd love a walk on the beach I washed up on," he said. "It'll be nice here, not having to be in a crowd."

"There'll be more people than I'm accustomed to. The population of my island has doubled. Let's go. I found a unique shell yesterday before you interrupted my walk. I want to retrieve it," she said eagerly.

"I'm sorry. That was rude of me. I'll be more considerate in the future." And off they went, side by side.

The serenity of the moment put them more at ease. They'd both revealed much of their past to the other. But they'd each recalled episodes in their lives that they'd laid aside. They'd lived life unaware of circumstances other than pursuing money. Each day, they'd file away the affairs of that day. They packed those affairs in a box and placed it on a storage shelf. Turning to walk away, they forgot the contents of the box. That shallow existence showed a common link in the friendship that was forming. The lessons learned by children growing up in a genuine, loving relationship manifest themselves as an adult in the delight of living. Each missed the first part as children. The delight of living was a concept foreign to the two islanders. They were getting a taste of it now.

Alex soon found her prize shell. "It's a horned helmet shell," she said proudly. "This species is one of the largest of the variety. It was most likely living on the coral reefs within our sight. They can fetch a couple of hundred dollars in the tourist market. I'd never sell it. It'll add well to my collection."

"You have a knowledge of shells," he observed.

"I found I needed something to do when I arrived here. Sitting in paradise was not enough. Without external stimulation on one's mind, the mind focuses within. I feared that. I occupied my time. This island's a small forested, rocky outcrop with coconut palms. I've explored parts of it. It's a conservation area for flying foxes, a species of large bats. The surrounding sea's a conservation area for sea turtles. Two professors at the National University of Samoa study these animals. I make observations and correspond with them through reports I give to Iosefa to post to them. They write me back. It's my contact with the outside world. They know nothing of my past. They pay me a stipend. I have my bank on the main island give it to Iosefa. It's another way I compensate him for what he does for me. My bank gives him a set amount each month from one of my accounts. He uses it to buy what I need. I'd guess he keeps part of it. People are the same everywhere. I ride back with him infrequently to take care of my affairs. I enjoy a night or two on the big island. He then brings me back. It's a good life."

Alex felt another wave wash over her again. This didn't trouble her as when the dam burst. The waves of judgment and sensibilities were having a cleansing effect on her. Each confession to Geoffrey felt like a cool shower after a hard day's work. It renewed her inner spirit like she didn't know was possible. She wanted to tell him more. She felt it was time to face her reality. But, as refreshing as it was, it caused her concern. She'd never been this open with anyone, even Phillip. She didn't know why she was now so drawn to Geoffrey. Something was stirring deep inside her. A good feeling and a bad one. Was she being enlightened, or was she like a moth being drawn to fire provided by Prometheus? Would she suffer the same fate as that Greek God? Would the seat of her human emotion be ripped out of her as it was with him? So much was provoking the perspectives she remembered from courses in social science and humanities when she was in college. Love, relationships, ideas, values, and creation were concepts being taught. She attended the classes, took the exams, and did what was necessary to pass. Finance was her focus then, not life lessons. She was getting the life lessons now, and she was being self-taught. This part troubled her. She'd nothing to gauge her feelings against. It was as if something greater than her thoughts were propelling her onward. Alex had much to learn. She knew a greater answer existed than the ones taught in those classes. She felt sure that Greek God didn't form her out of clay. She sensed a more profound answer was waiting.

Alex continued speaking. "Geoffrey, when I left the states, I wanted to go nowhere, the same as you. I wanted a remote island in the middle of the Pacific Ocean. I picked Samoa and bought a one-way plane ticket. Once I was in Samoa, I found this island. With enough money, anything is possible. I had enough money. I made things happen. I bought a piece of this island, had this house built, and spent the first year forgetting my past. Once I accomplished that, I enjoyed my new life. I was living in the present until you washed up. You're my past in many ways. No one can ever run away forever. Maybe I thought I enjoyed the life I had in the states. I regret the way I made my money. I can't change that, and giving it back would achieve nothing. This is who I am. I live with it now on this island."

Geoffrey spoke. "It's a life of most people's dreams. And you found it by running away. It seems, besides a shell collector, you're quite the philosopher," he noted. "I can see your point of view. I can also see why you are at peace here. Anyone could be. I know I could be." He waited. Her response would tell him much.

"We came here for a walk," she said as she proceeded along the beach. He soon caught up to her and walked by her side. He knew he shouldn't say anything else. The next move would be hers.

6

It was another typical day on an island in this region of the Pacific. The temperature barely changes here. It was summer, which only meant it wasn't as rainy as the winter months. Seasons in this part of the world feel the same. One would only think of them when looking at a calendar. Alex hadn't looked at a calendar in years. She hadn't looked at a clock either. It was because she had neither. She felt no sense of time; there was only day and night. During the day, she lived; during the night, she slept. Today wasn't unlike every day, except she had a man beside her. Trade winds wafted over them. It was stimulating. The coastline under their feet was rejuvenating. The couple on the beach felt more alive than either of them could remember. Neither understood why.

Was it this island? he thought.

Could it be my companion? she pondered.

They each concluded it was the release of dormant emotions.

There might have been another reason. Was it a latent attraction to someone of the opposite sex? It wasn't as they'd experienced with someone else in their prior years. This was distinctively not the same. Each desired to be with the other. It came to the two minds concurrently. Each turned to gaze at the one beside them. As their eyes met, they both turned back quickly, refocusing on the shore ahead.

Alex was in a new world. Her island, she thought now, appeared so diverse today. She looked up at the lush green hillside. Where she once saw a forest, she now saw individual trees. An enormous banyan tree dominated the hillside beside her. Loulu palms intermingled with the ever-present coconut palms as if companions. The enormous umbrella-like canopy of a koa tree seemed to hover over a section of the undergrowth. She realized there was a Cananga tree on her island. Finding one growing this far from the western Pacific islands was unusual. And, of course, the ever-present banana trees were her source of fruit not provided by Iosefa. He'd taught her the flora of the island when she first arrived. She'd listened. Her mind was on more depressing things back then. Now his lessons were as if he spoke them yesterday. There were many species of lush green vegetation under the many trees. They appeared as many as the grains of sand under her feet. Viewing the scene brought back memories of her childhood in spring. The grounds of the estate where she lived as a child were nature's palette. The gardener had always created such stunning rainbows of color with his flowers and shrubs. It was one of the bright spots in her life as a little girl. *What a waste*, she thought. No one in her family comprehended it. Then it occurred to her. *The gardener did!* It affirmed many rationalizations she'd come to recently. Beauty was everywhere in her life. She'd never appreciated it until now. That gardener had a wonderful life. He lived a dream every day. His pay was adequate, she was sure. *His life was richer than mine then,* she thought.

She turned her gaze to the crystal clear water. The vivid colors of the living coral reef were as she remembered her gardener's landscape painting. The coral shared its colors with the fish. Each mimicked the other. She saw the exquisiteness in her world and her life. It was everywhere. It was now a reality. This island had been a place to escape. Beauty wasn't only now in her sight; it was in her mind. For the first time since her arrival, she'd discussed and faced her emotions. Now that they were out, she sensed a weight she'd been carrying had left. It created a wonderful feeling. She felt happy.

She'd been walking beside Geoffrey on the inland side. She looked at him. He was staring out over the water. *I'm glad he washed up on my island*, she thought. *He's no Prince Charming, but I wasn't Cinderella either. We've similar backgrounds. On the surface, he's somewhat likeable. We're going to be together for a while. I may as well enjoy the company. At least it'll be a change.*

"Do you like to fish?" she asked.

Delighted she was starting a conversation, he answered, "I never had much time for it. I'd one client with a large boat. He'd asked me to go along with him twice. He even let me take it out by myself once. I've been on a couple of deepwater fishing trips with clients. I was more focused on schmoozing them than fishing."

"Well, here it's not a social activity. I do it because I don't like to eat canned soup or dried beans. The waters around the island are teeming with dinner. I've snorkels, masks, fins, and spearguns. I keep two of everything. I need to have spares. I can't run to the store if something breaks."

"Sounds good to me. You'll have to teach me."

"I'll teach you how to use the speargun. The rest involves breathing and moving your legs. It appears you've mastered that."

"I'm ready whenever you are."

The new friends turned and walked toward the cabin.

Geoffrey didn't have the perspicacity to recognize what was happening to Alex. He'd realized that intellectually she was his better. She was emotionally his superior as well. He wasn't even sure what was happening to him. The clear-sightedness of his feelings had escaped him. But he knew something was stirring in his self-consciousness. He valued her compassion, generosity, benevolence, and kindness. It went beyond his gratitude. He was aware of the sum of what Alex had done for him in the hours he'd known her. He was now keenly mindful of its value to him. It surpassed anything anyone other than his parents had ever done for him. *Why? Why was she doing this for him?* He knew himself, and he didn't deserve this. The clarity returned to his thoughts. *She was giving,* he concluded. One rarely gave to him, and he to others. Still, he recognized the fact. He received a gift from Alex. He felt a new emotional awareness. It created a twinge of humility. He knew it was real. Pride and arrogance had left him. He'd been so full of himself with his evil deeds and ill-gotten gains. Their value was worthless on this island. His only possession was his self-worth. Its value was a trifle as he appraised his new friend's worth. He realized the island his life had been. It was much smaller than the one he was on now. Then it hit him like a thunderbolt. The gift he'd received was of such a great value to him. Something this precious was not his to have in his earlier existence. It was a gift of great worth. She'd told him she wanted to be his friend! No one had ever said that. No one had ever wanted that. His previous acquaintances knew his shallowness. So did Alex, but she overlooked it. He now had a friend! An excitement came over him; he stopped to control himself.

Alex stopped beside him. "What's the matter? You've a strange look on your face. Are you feeling okay?"

He told the truth. "I don't think I've ever felt better. Alex, I've thanked you many times for what you've done for me. I said you'd only hear the truth from me. I want to tell you now. I especially want to thank you for being my friend."

She saw the look on his face. She could read facial expressions. The one she saw spoke sincerity. "Thank you, Geoffrey. You have your faults. Maybe you're a sweet man. Let's get our equipment. I have to teach you how to survive out here." They continued the walk back into the cabin.

7

Upon arriving inside the cabin, Alex stated, "You'll have to use your shorts as your swim pants," she said. "I'll change into my swimsuit and get the gear. Give me a minute."

Geoffrey felt like a schoolboy. He was going out with a girl who liked him. They were going out together as friends. It'd be fair to say he felt lighthearted. It was as if he'd arrived at her house for a date. He was sitting on her couch, nervously awaiting her entrance into the room.

Alex returned with the equipment. When Geoffrey saw her, he was that young schoolboy. *Wow!* entered his mind. She was wearing a modest two-piece swimsuit. He knew she was an attractive woman. Now he knew she had the body to match her face.

This is going to be the best date…fishing trip…I've ever been on! he thought.

"Let me help you with the gear. I'll carry it for you!" he blurted.

"You carry the spearguns and snorkel equipment. I'll take the towels and water." They proceeded out the door.

The event excited the pair. Neither had felt this much enthusiasm. During the walk to the beach, each glanced at the other. The observation by the observer created a warm feeling for each. It was because each knew that which was observed was a friend.

Walking toward the beach, Alex said, "The snorkel is easy, just breathe naturally. When you go under, hold your breath. When you surface, blow through your snorkel to clear the water. You'll need to adjust the strap on your goggles. It needs to fit tight against your face. Don't push too hard with your legs, just a smooth, consistent motion. Let the flippers do the work." Alex realized she was speaking slowly. She was speaking to teach. She wanted Geoffrey to enjoy the event. This was a different Alex. She wasn't controlling him. She was just with him. It felt good to her.

When they reached the water's edge, they put down their equipment.

"Take one speargun. I need to show you how to use it. Stand beside me." She took one speargun in her hand, and he did the same. "Put the base of the gun against your chest. Pull the rubber strap with both hands back until you can place it in the notch above the trigger." He followed her movements and did as she showed him.

"That's easy," he said.

"Remember, these are deadly guns. Keep them pointed away from us. You'll need to be within twelve feet of your prey when shooting. Pull the trigger like you would on a pistol, and we'll have dinner. I'll point at the fish to shoot." They put on their gear and went into the water.

They lingered over the surface, looking through the transparent water. Alex had done this many times. It was always a stunning scene. The diversity of the coral and the collage of colors, made each trip special. Each swim seemed like the first. She once tried to keep track of the different species of fish she encountered. She soon gave that up. Today was different and much more special than any earlier visit. She was aware of the fact she wasn't alone. This thought brought a joy to her heart. She hadn't felt this for many years. It bewildered her how her isolation had been an enjoyment until now. The companionship of Geoffrey was like a piece of cake on her birthday. It was a pleasure, remembered and long forgotten. Maybe, just maybe, she'd gotten it wrong. Had she run so far that she'd run past what sustained her? They must supply an army in battle. A soul needs nourishment on its journey through life. Alex had outrun that which supplied her. She couldn't define it. But she sensed it now; she was malnourished. She was feasting on that which her soul required. The coconuts could grow and thrive on this island by themselves. It was becoming obvious to her she could not.

She realized her companion wasn't near her. She saw him slipping through the water. He was at least twenty yards away. She swam over to him and tapped him on the shoulder. It startled him, and his body jerked. She had turned upright in the water. He did the same.

Removing her snorkel from her mouth, she said, "Good thing I stopped you. You were going toward the other island."

"I'm sorry." He had the look of wonder as a child entering the tent of his first circus. "I was in another world. I've never seen such beautiful sights in my life. It's fascinating!" What he said struck a chord in him. Beauty was something he recognized. Splendid things had been in his life. He'd once been too busy with matters now trivial to acknowledge their existence. He'd learned a life lesson. His awakening was transpiring along with Alexandria's. Money should be seen as an object, not a lifestyle, if one wants to witness the emotional capacity that lies within us. The joy of this moment was priceless to Geoffrey. Each was aware that they had achieved so little in life at the expense of so much.

"I know," she responded. "I still get the same feeling each time. Let's get a couple of fish for dinner. We can come back and do what you were doing."

"Okay. Lead the way."

Alex started moving through the water with her pupil a few feet behind her. She searched for an excellent fish for her friend to spear. Spotting a blotcheye soldierfish, she pointed her spear toward it. She then pointed her finger at him. He knew she was motioning for him to shoot it. Starting toward it, he felt her hand on his leg. He turned to see her motioning him to slow. They cautiously approached the prey. When Geoffrey was within ten feet, she gestured like she was pulling a trigger. He pointed the gun at the fish and pulled the trigger. The spear hit its center. He dove the few feet under the surface and retrieved his prize.

Coming to the surface, they removed their snorkels. "I did it!" the hunter shouted with enthusiasm.

"Good shot," his guide said. "You follow me. We'll head toward the beach, and I'll get another fish along the way." It only took a minute for her to spot a surgeon fish. She speared it, retrieved it, and motioned for him to head to the beach. Once on the beach, they removed their equipment. Geoffrey couldn't contain his excitement.

He blurted out, "I don't think I've ever had so much fun. That was a fantastic adventure. Thanks for letting me do this with you."

"I'm happy for you. I still enjoy it each time I get my dinner this way. I enjoyed it even more today."

For a few heartbeats, they stood on this deserted beach looking at each other. To each, nothing existed at this moment. Their eyes peered into the other's. Each experienced the same sensation. They were of the same mind. The emotional pull of the other was becoming pronounced. It was like the gravitational relationship between the earth and the moon. They were in harmonious balance. They would lose the equilibrium if one took more than the other gave. If so, they would go off in separate directions. The island companions were finding this, which neither even knew existed only days ago, could flourish in themselves. The start of a genuine friendship was strengthening. They were finding this balance. Love was starting.

Alex broke the momentary trance. "I saw a Samoan crab. Tomorrow we'll come back and try to find one. It's a real delicacy. Do you want to go back as a tourist? We have our dinner."

"I'd love that."

"Okay. Remember to look to see where you are. I won't swim out into the ocean to retrieve you."

"I wouldn't expect you to. Let's go."

The confidants spent the rest of the morning enjoying their swim. They shared the perception of a wonderful time with the other. It created a special feeling. Geoffrey couldn't recall such a moment in his life. The thrill to him was beyond any dream he may have had, if he had dreamed. But the wonders he was finding now were real. Alex had these feelings long ago. They seemed like a dream. To her, whether they had been real or a dream, she didn't remember them to be this wonderful. She wasn't aware of ever giving so much of herself to anyone before her intimate arrived on her island.

Geoffrey was feeling emotions he hadn't felt before his arrival from his previous island to his current island. He was seeing sights he'd never seen. He didn't want to get out of the water. It was mesmerizing to him. Alex felt the same revelation she'd felt walking on the beach and seeing her island for the first time. She was seeing the water world as she'd not seen it until this swim. She'd a sense of seeing things differently now. And it wasn't just the coral reef.

After a while, they made their way toward the beach. Out of the water, they removed their snorkeling equipment and looked at each other. A smile came to their faces. It'd been a good day. It wasn't finished.

"I've never caught my dinner. This fish will be better than the last. You're an excellent cook." Then the thought occurred to him. "I'm sorry. I'm assuming you'll prepare dinner again. Forgive me. I shouldn't be so presumptuous."

"That's okay. I planned on doing it. But thanks for saying that," she replied.

"Show me how to prepare the fish. I'll do that part. I'm a quick learner."

"Deal. Let's get back to the cabin. We can get cleaned up and enjoy the afternoon on the deck. The rain shower last night supplied us with enough water for us to shower. I have more wine." She grabbed part of the equipment; he gathered the rest.

Proudly carrying the fish on the spears, he looked at them as he walked back. When not looking at the fish, he couldn't take his eyes off of Alex. *What an incredible woman! Of all the beaches to wash up on…!"* he speculated.

After they had both showered, they prepared their feast. Geoffrey had cleaned the fish while Alex prepared the rest of the meal. It was a delightful evening for the two, each thinking what an energizing time they were having. Each hoped the day wouldn't end. But it did. Retiring for the night, they shared the same thought. *This was one of the best days of my life!*

8

*T*he young girl looked fabulous in her floral calico dress, her long hair trailing behind her in the breeze. A glow on her face spoke of the blissfulness she was feeling. The gallant young man holding the reins had the horse at a steady trot. The creaking and flexing of the buckboard was a joyous sound to the couple. He could never use it for such a purpose until today. She turned her head toward him. How handsome he looked, *she thought. In all her junior years, she had dreamed of a day such as this. This dream was ever present on her mind. But most young girls had this same dream. Someone would introduce a boy to her. He'd call on her one Sunday afternoon at her home. Then he'd meet her parents. He'd ask her to go on a picnic with him. She'd then fall in love, they'd marry, and live happily ever after. It made lives from dreams such as this.*

"How about over there?" he said, pointing at the large oak tree just off the dirt road.

"That's perfect," she cooed.

Hopping out of the seat, she bounded over the grass, pirouetting around and dancing to the yapping of the small dog beside her. Reaching down, she grabbed a handful of blue asters; they stretched endlessly across the meadow. Looking around, she noticed all of nature. The prairie grass stood tall against the gentle breeze. A low, booming sound of a prairie chicken calling for a mate was ever present. The blue sky with its puffs of white was the arena for the birds dancing in the air. They were singing only for her. God created all this for me, *she thought. Twirling around, she saw her companion sitting on a blue-and-white checkered tablecloth lying on the ground. Spread before him was a feast of chicken, corn, bread, and pie. "I'm so glad we came," she purred as she made her way toward him. She imagined she was walking on air. "Tell me you love me," she murmured, as she knelt beside him. She peered into his dreamy eyes as he gazed upon her face and smiled.*

* * *

Suddenly, a loud crash rang out!

Startled, Alex sat up straight in bed. Rising quickly, she put on her robe and went into the kitchen. There she saw Geoffrey bending over broken shards of a plate on the floor. He had the look of a small child in the same situation, and his mother was staring at him.

"Geoffrey, what on earth are you doing?" she stated.

"I wanted to fix you breakfast and surprise you," he answered sheepishly. "So much for the surprise."

"That was part of my best Walmart service for eight. I got it on sale for $19.95." Alex was trying her best not to laugh out loud.

"Maybe we can order a replacement," Geoffrey responded, smiling.

"No, forget it. I'll just have to do without. I guess I'll need to teach you how to handle dishes too."

"It's obvious I need it."

"I ruined the surprise, but I'll not ruin your preparing me breakfast. How long will it take for it to be ready, assuming you break nothing else?"

"About fifteen minutes."

"I'll get dressed and be back in fifteen," Alex answered. Turning, she went back into her room. The smile on her face and the joy in her heart announced her feelings. *He's fixing me breakfast. No one's ever done that before*, she thought.

As she looked in her mirror, she couldn't comprehend how she could have changed so much over the days since Geoffrey arrived. The sometimes sad, sometimes hopeful face she'd seen was gone. There was a radiance to her complexion now that was fascinating.

Her eyes sparkled. *Something happened to you, Alex,* she thought to herself. *Why had this stranger caused such a change in my attitude?*

Something in Alex, having lain dormant until now, was blossoming. Just as a seed needs the right soil, climate conditions, and water to sprout and grow, so love needs certain things. We are born with the ability to love. Within each person, love exists to be given. The ability to give love is limitless. The capacity to receive love is boundless. Love blossoms when one's life meets the right person, at the right time, in the right place. Such a profound event of such an unexplainable nature must be part of a greater plan. He created us for a purpose, made to fulfill that purpose. Alex had begun this new journey. She was feeling the unwavering passion that was to become her daily companion.

She knew she was in a new world, a world in which she was unacquainted. It created a twinge of sadness. She realized things that never happened could have happened. This thought created a sense of loss. She knew she had been alive. For the first time, she knew she had never lived life. It was as if time made an error and was correcting itself now. Now she was living as many others had lived every day of their lives. Alex knew she was falling in love. But one thought troubled her. *Am I falling in love with Geoffrey, or am I falling in love with love?*

I'll put on a little makeup this morning, she thought. *I want to look my best.* The woman had only the minimum. It was all she needed or wanted. A light touch of blush, one brush of mascara, and a complimentary lip color were enough. After putting on a nicer blouse than her regular T-shirt, she brushed her hair. Checking herself in the mirror, she proceeded into the kitchen.

She noticed he set the table in a complete setting for two. The breakfast aroma drifted through the room. She didn't see any of the utensils needed to prepare the meal. The kitchen was clean. The food and coffee were on the table. *He washed and put up the pots and pans,* she thought. The exhilaration of the moment created an atmosphere of almost zero gravity. She seemed to float as she approached Geoffrey.

"Well, it's obvious you have one talent you haven't mentioned. You know your way around a kitchen. It appears as if you had the meal catered," the lady exclaimed joyfully.

"I've always enjoyed eating good food. It was one of my few pleasures of my earlier life. I cooked for myself, sometimes for a few friends," the chef replied.

"You even cleaned the kitchen. You're an organized person. I guess I was wrong about you. You have at least two redeeming qualities."

"Sit. Let's eat before it gets cold."

Sitting, Alex spoke. "That looks spectacular. What is it?"

"It's a frittata. I saw onions, mushrooms, and other vegetables. You had enough eggs left and a little ham. I'm afraid I used up most of those. I hope you don't mind. We may have to survive on coconuts and fish until your supply boat returns."

"Geoffrey, you did too much! Thank you for doing this. It was very thoughtful."

"It's the least I can do after all you've done for me."

Geoffrey poured coffee into each of their cups. Smiling at him, she took a bite of her meal. "I stand corrected. You're up to three redeeming qualities now. You're an experienced cook. This is delicious!"

"I'm glad. I'm sorry it cost you a plate."

"Keep cooking like this and you can drop a plate on the floor every time."

Continuing her breakfast, mixed with light conversation, Alex couldn't take her eyes off her confidant. For the first time since arriving on her island, something separated her from her past. It was as if her life began when she found Geoffrey on the beach. No prior recollection of life came to her mind. So much had happened since that moment. Alex was feeling something she had felt previously. But even then, it was only superficial. For the first time, Alex was aware of fallow passions. This man across the table from her had regenerated them. She knew it wasn't just the man. It was the way he treated her. He regarded her in ways no one ever had. She comprehended these feelings even though no one taught them to her. She understood them as if something inside of her longed for them, and now they had manifested themselves for her. Pondering what she knew of Geoffrey, her earlier opinion of him dimmed with the grasp of the true nature of the man. His redeeming qualities were becoming too many to count. She saw what she didn't see when they first met. He possessed what she wanted. He cared for her, understood her, respected her, validated her, and affirmed her. Every woman wants these sensibilities in a man. Given these by Geoffrey, Alex felt something she longed for. Alex felt like a woman falling in love. Savoring every bite and each minute, she didn't want the meal to end.

Geoffrey was captivated by the moment as well. Unlike Alex, he was continually thinking of days gone by. Each glance at his incredible dining companion turned any thought of a past event into triviality. As each person in his past came to mind, the clarity of their shallowness became pronounced. He felt his entire life had been a journey to reach this point with her. He was as perplexed as Alex. How could such a random event occur to such perfection? He knew there was an explanation, but he didn't dwell on it. His mind's focus was on his housemate.

What a gorgeous, intelligent, vibrant person she is, and she seems to enjoy my company, he thought.

But something more profound was stirring inside. He was experiencing sensations not discerned before this moment. Any male chauvinist attitude he had didn't exist in him on this island. His encounter with Alex created a commonality of spirit and purpose. It was unique to his life. Not a man given to introspection, he still realized Alex had become a close friend. But he knew it went beyond the elucidation of a friend. He was witnessing emotions long held deep within brought forth. These emotions involved sharing and caring. In the past, he'd neither shared with nor cared about anyone else, unless it would help himself. He did these things with Alex because he wanted to give to her. He wasn't as perceptive about his emotions as Alex was with hers. But he knew he had a special feeling for her. He'd not grasped the concept of love. But he knew his feelings for her were special, and these feelings didn't exist in his consciousness before meeting her.

The two diners eventually finished their meal. Engrossed in their conversation, neither of them was aware of doing it. They couldn't take their eyes off the other. The couple was relishing their new world with each moment.

9

Alex spoke. "Let's go exploring the island together. I walked parts of it when I first moved here. I wasn't a happy camper then and found no enjoyment in it. But it will be different with you now," she said with a twinkle in her eyes.

"I'd love that. You'd better change. I'm sure we'll be in a thick brush. My total wardrobe is right," he observed.

Alex left the room and returned wearing hiking clothes and boots. She carried a machete. Handing the machete to Geoffrey, she said, "You carry this. We may need it."

They went along the beach of the cove. Coming upon Geoffrey's life jacket, they realized they'd forgotten it. Picking it up, she tossed it into the underbrush. "Sometimes tourists come to this cove not knowing anyone lives here. They never stay long. But they may tell someone of this," she said. The explorers proceeded along the beach and past the end of the cove.

"This is the way up this side of the rocks and trees. There's evidence of an old path. I never made it very far. Iosefa told me long ago the natives buried the high chiefs of Manono on this island. I'm not sure where," Alex told her companion.

Geoffrey took the lead. Occasionally, rocks seemed to have been placed purposely up the steep hill. Geoffrey swung the machete to remove the intermittent fern that had grown up in the path. The adventurers made it to the summit, if one could call it that. Rocks at the highest point on the island were only fifty meters above the ocean. The vantage point showed the geography of the island. It was obvious it was impractical to venture into the brush anywhere else on the island. The sandy shore and the cove where Alex had her cabin built were one of the few places one could enjoy this pile of volcanic rock. They exerted considerable effort to come this far. They wanted to stay and enjoy the view. The vast expanse of blue-green water took on a different perspective from what the observers had standing on the beach. The two large islands of Samoa, Upolu and Savai'i, were visible on either side of their vantage point.

"I'm glad we came, Geoffrey. Standing here gives me a new perception of my home and my world. It gives me a new opinion of my life. I live on an island, but maybe I'm not the island I thought I was," Alex confided.

Looking into her eyes, Geoffrey replied, "I sense the same understanding in myself since I met you. I only want to live for the moment. We navigated life differently, but our courses brought us to the same place. Maybe it's not where one is in life that's important. Maybe it's who you have beside you."

Suddenly, Alex felt overcome with empathy and compassion. She understood and shared Geoffrey's experiences and emotions, and felt sorrow for what he'd missed or misunderstood about his life experiences. A large part of her life had paralleled his. She also felt something awakening inside of her, a quality never used to describe her. It wasn't temporal. It would be part of her new relationship. Gentleness was now part of her emotional composition. Prior traits of her personality were washing away within the tide of change happening with her. They were being replaced with what she needed in this new arena of life. The truly feminine side of Alex, long suppressed, was emerging. Her adventures with the sojourner in her life were a new collection. It replaced the one of her shells. She was now collecting that which the soul finds most valuable—emotional experiences. She was learning to understand how unique each was.

With a calm and softened voice, Alex spoke. "Geoffrey, I sense a purpose and meaning to life that goes beyond the boundaries of our world. What is time? What is life? Maybe nothing ever dies. It only changes. I know I've changed since I arrived on this island. I've changed since you arrived on this island. I feel created for a purpose. There's a sense that I'm on a road to fulfilling that purpose and an unwavering passion never felt. This creates so many questions. I guess our answers lie in our own fate."

Once again, Geoffrey was aware of the power of Alex's emotions. It showed in her speech and new demeanor. Once again, he realized how superior she was to him. Her insight and kindheartedness were off the scale compared to his. She awed him, and it awakened an emotion in him. It was to erupt like a long-dormant volcano. Love was swelling up inside of him. He could not define it, but he felt its volume growing in him. All it needed was a spark.

Not capable of responding to her, he simply looked into her eyes and held her hands. "You're one incredible woman, Alex," he said. "Let's go back to the beach."

With a gentle squeeze of her hand, she said, "Okay."

One last glance at the Pacific Ocean, and they walked down the rocky hillside. With Geoffrey in the lead and Alex following, they slowly made their way along the path. They were deep in thought, but Alex was more so. Her mind and heart were twirling in joyous celebration. She could never remember feeling the thrill she was experiencing at the moment. This momentary thrill would end in a split second.

The path down the hill was barely as wide as a human body. Path makers had cut it out of the steep hillside at this point near the summit. The hillside was on Alex's right side. A sharp drop-off was to her left. With her mind not focusing on her footsteps, it was inevitable. Landing on loose rocks, her left foot gave way down the hillside. Her balance lost, she tipped over the side. She screamed!

"Geoffrey!"

The sense of panic was evident in her voice. Geoffrey turned instantly to see her, only a few feet away, tipping over toward the forest below. His brain responded as designed. In a split second, his body reacted to the adrenaline rush as his heart pushed it through his veins. His legs sprang forward to catch her. But her situation was progressing as fast as his response. She at once sensed that she must stop her motion away from the hillside. As her left foot gave way, she knew she had to twist her body, so it'd face the hillside and she could use her hands to stop her fall. But in turning her body, her right foot slides down as well. Both feet were off the path and going down the side. She reached out with both hands to grab the ground.

To Geoffrey, everything was happening in slow motion. And to his horror, his motions were a split second behind those of Alex's. As he lunged forward to grab her, her body was slipping away. He threw his weight forward to land where she was. His arms strained to grab her. Instinctively, she reached out her left hand to grab his outstretched arm. This lessened her delicate hold of the ground and further advanced her fall. Geoffrey's body hit the path, his outstretched hand inches away from hers. The pain from his chest hitting the rocks was excruciating. At the moment, he ignored it. Geoffrey's response was at its limit.

Alex's momentum was now in control. As her hands on the path could not hold her weight, they slid with the rest of her body. She let out a piercing scream of terror. The sound branded its imprint in Geoffrey's mind forever.

As Alex's arms lost their hold on the mountain, they instinctively flailed out, away from her body. Her left arm hit a small tree growing out of the side of the hill. She bent her arm around it to stop her progress toward the trees and ground below. Her slide stopped for a split second. She reached over and grabbed the thin trunk with her right hand. It had abated her fall. Then there was a cracking sound. The small piece of wood fiber couldn't sustain her weight. She slipped again a little further toward the tree canopy twenty meters away

The moment Geoffrey had hit the ground, he immediately sprang forward to reach Alex. With his body extended over the side as far as he realized safe, he reached out to grab her. He could not touch her. She was only inches away.

"Alex!" he shouted. He wanted to pull her back with his voice.

If the frail support holding her snapped again, she'd be gone. Each did the only thing they could. Geoffrey pushed himself further than he thought safe. Alex released her right hand from the failing hold on her life. They each looked at the other. The fixation of their eyes on the other was a bond not to be broken.

It became a moment frozen in time. It created an indelible mark on their memories, never to be erased. All the emotions in the cauldron of their psyche poured out into their consciousness. It's as if the brain senses an end and releases its contents. They were instantly aware of the essence of how they felt about each other. The instantaneous sense of losing this may have been the deciding factor.

Seemingly beyond their limits, the outstretched hand of each touched the other. Geoffrey grasped Alex's hand. It was secure. Intuitively, they reached out with their other hand to grasp their counterpart. Geoffrey now had control of Alex. He pulled her over the side onto the path. The adrenaline ceasing and the pain increasing brought a stillness for a few seconds. As they each rose on their knees, Alex couldn't control herself. Shaking uncontrollably, she reached out and hugged Geoffrey. Her scared arms clutched him so hard it was as if she wanted to be absorbed into him. Tears of terror and joy flowed down her face. She couldn't stop sobbing.

Geoffrey didn't know a body could feel the relief he felt. He had done the impossible. He couldn't understand how it happened or how he did it. It didn't matter at the moment. He was holding Alex in his arms. He realized he had never felt better in his life. For an instant, he had lost the best thing to happen to him. Somehow, the event had been reversed. He felt invigorated by the realization of the finality. He knew there was no mistaking his feeling for Alex. He knew what he felt, although he could not describe it. Defining it, he knew it was love.

After a few moments, Alex regained her composure. She relaxed her grip on the man who had saved her life. As she pulled back, she gazed upon the face she knew she loved. A fresh wave swept over her. It wasn't like any earlier wave. This one created a sense of euphoria never experienced. Love does that to a person.

10

Each was secure in the loving arms of the other. Geoffrey's fall badly bruised his chest. Scrapes on Alex's legs and arms were many. They felt nothing of this. Only what was now a fire burning in their hearts. Two people who fall in love create an intoxicating experience. It must be lived to be understood. No one is conversant with every relationship. Each happening creates a uniqueness. What was happening to Alex and Geoffrey was beyond their rationalization. Their lips met. The feeling far surpassed any they had ever experienced. It stirred up feelings of affection and attachment. The emotional bond between them was complete now.

His enraptured embrace ignited a flurry of thoughts in Geoffrey. *I have the love, respect, and acceptance of one special person, the one I love. The love and respect of the rest of the world isn't necessary. I once sought that along with the accumulation of money. I sought it in an unknown world. It can reject me now. It doesn't matter. A few moments ago, I almost lost that special person. She validates everything that I am. She is my world now. For an instant, I thought I'd lost her. I've never been in love before now. I don't know if all men feel the same.*

His mind envisioned everything about her, and he shut out all else. The shape of her face, the way her smile accents her face, the glow of her eyes, the size of her hand in his. He peered deep into her eyes and felt the beauty he beheld draw him into the depths of her soul. He ceased to be standing before her; he was now part of her. He sensed he couldn't untangle his being from hers even if he had been ordered to do so. He saw her now, as if he'd always known her. What a change love makes in a man. What a magnificent secret he carries with him. The tender passions come out of his heart. He loves as a bird sings or as a flower blossoms. He realizes love isn't something one learns. It's because love comes from the heart, not the mind.

Many people wait for true love. Some people wait and continue waiting. Or they try to create in another individual what they have fantasized about all their lives. Then, when it doesn't work out, they can't understand what went wrong. A power beyond this world plans and creates perfect matches. We cannot create them.

The thread being woven into Alex when Geoffrey came into her life was strong. It bound every part of her to him. Alex had dreamed of ethereal, idyllic relationships and feelings. Once there was a cold and calculating nature to her. She had always been a woman. She'd never seen examples of her dreams and knew so little about them. She now knew what was important. Genuine love is an action, not just a feeling. It produces sacrificial giving. The greatest act of love is giving oneself to another. He'd risk his life to save her. She knew such a thing as a perfect match existed. She didn't need a bolt of light to show her. She knew love. It's not something that's part of a being grown from a primordial pool. Instincts and some emotions may be born from DNA. But love is beyond emotions. It's *placed* in everyone. It's the source and purpose of our creation. The Creator prepared what Alex and Geoffrey were experiencing for the union of them.

"Can you stand?" Geoffrey asked as he looked at her battered body.

"I'm shaking so much. Just a moment." Alex sensed she had not been breathing normally. She was only at this moment catching her breath. She was now aware of the pain in parts of her body.

"Oh, Geoffrey! I've never felt such fear in my life. I thought I was going to fall all the way." She took a deep breath. "It happened so fast."

"I know. You were only inches away. I felt so helpless. I'll never know how I could grab your hand."

"Geoffrey, so many thoughts have been going through my mind since we met. Each moment I'm with you is better than the preceding. Something's happening to me. I can't explain it, but I know it's real. It's like I found what I sensed was always missing in my life. I know what I feel for you. I know what it is. I've found true love, Geoffrey. And I wasn't looking for it! I feel I had written my life on a sheet of paper. Somehow, someone cut off the part before you arrived and threw it away, as if it never existed. I only want to be with you." Alex realized she was speaking as she never had. She was now a new Alex. The commanding, conquering woman of power had vanished. She couldn't find words to describe how she felt. But she knew how she felt. She was a consummate woman. "I love you, Geoffrey. My love for you isn't asking you to change. I'm only inviting you into a safe place where you can stop pretending. True love doesn't ask you to change. It simply invites."

Geoffrey could feel his heart pounding. "Alex, my heart has never felt such a flame. There've been moments since I met you when I stopped breathing in your presence. I want to see beautiful sights. I want to look into your eyes. I want to see me in your eyes. My past journey shouldn't dictate my fresh path. Every tomorrow that comes, you'll be a part of my today. Many questions have gone unanswered. Love's given me the answers. We found something on this path today. We've taken other paths in our lives. There's only one that matters. It's the path of love. I think we're on that path and it's good. I'm kneeling before you just as a man. A man looking at a woman, telling her he loves her."

Their eyes peered deep into the others. Their lips met with the soft caress of a mother on her newborn child. The euphoria of the embrace dulled the sensory pathways of the brain. The feelings of the flesh weren't active in their minds. Something placed in their subconscious at a time beyond comprehension had become the guiding force in their lives.

Their sense of awareness now focused on their injuries. Although not incapacitating, they were significant. Forces of nature made this island with volcanic rock. Worn by the elements, it was nonetheless far from smooth. They realized they were both bleeding. They did not see imminent danger but needed to return to the cabin to treat their injuries. Geoffrey helped Alex to her feet.

Turning his back to her, he said, "Put your arms around my waist. I'll start slowly with my right foot. You move your legs in lockstep with mine. We're going to be very careful." She did as he instructed. Cautiously, they proceeded down the hillside. Once at the bottom, he turned toward her and smiled. "I don't want to go there again!"

His smile brought a smile to her face as well. A sense of security came to them. She joined him at the moment. "I think I'll let you plan our next adventure. I make bad choices. Let's confine our excursions to sand and water."

Putting his right arm around her, he held her left hand with his. Having her securely in his grasp, he said, "Let's go home."

Upon entering the cabin, Geoffrey walked his new responsibility over to the kitchen table. Pulling out a chair, he helped her sit. He took a glass of water to Alex. "Where are the medical supplies? I'll get them."

"There, in a small box on the top shelf of the cabinet in the bathroom. Get a couple of bowls out from the kitchen cabinet. We'll use them to clean our scrapes."

He assembled the items. Alex, always prepared, had everything they needed. It took some time, but they cleaned and bandaged where needed. With the antiseptics and painkillers that were available, they were soon feeling none the worse for wear. They each realized how the event had drained them physically and emotionally.

"Let's go rest on the couch," he suggested.

"I'm thinking the same," she answered.

Stiffness settled in on the two adventurers. Gingerly, they made their way to the couch. Geoffrey sat and motioned for her to sit beside him. She sat, leaning her body next to his as he put his arm around her shoulders. He laid his head back on the couch. She placed her head against his shoulder. In a moment, they were both asleep.

11

S ometime later, Alex moved and then moaned. She realized her body felt as inflexible as a board. Given the adrenaline- and terror-induced state she was in earlier, she only now realized the strain it had placed on every muscle in her body. She thought she couldn't get up off the couch. Her agitation stirred Geoffrey out of his slumber. He felt the same as Alex, maybe worse. Each breath he took was painful. He opened his shirt and saw the bruising of his chest had worsened. She turned to look at his battered body.

"Geoffrey, that looks bad. Are you okay?"

"Inhaling hurts. I must have bruised or cracked some ribs when I hit the ground."

"Oh, Geoffrey! I wish there was more I could do for you." Heartfelt compassion was dripping from her words.

"I'm feeling pain when breathing, but I can tolerate it. It's not an option. I'm sure it'll get better in a few days. Other than a few scrapes, this is my only problem. Looking at you, though. You're a mess!" he said with a grin.

She broke out with a laugh. It hurt to laugh. She laughed again anyway. "I was going to change into something nice. I don't think I'll bother now." Reflecting, the new Alex spoke. "Geoffrey, life is so different now for many reasons. At the moment, I love laughing at life with you. I've never laughed at life like this. I fought it, cried because of it, ran from it, thought I could control it. I never enjoyed it. I'm enjoying it now more than I could have ever dreamed of. You make me laugh! I see life through a fresh set of lenses now. My sight is clear, crystal clear. With you, life is real."

"We need to eat. I'll prepare something simple. You need to rest. My hurts are temporal. By tomorrow, I hope I'll be mobile. I'll open our last bottle of wine. I think it'll serve us well tonight for many reasons."

And so the evening went. Alex prepared a nourishing meal. The couple could have been dining on prime rib or Spam, they wouldn't have known which. Their senses focused on the other and the events of the day. They had forever branded two unique experiences into their memory. The dramatic events of Alex's rescue would be told and retold throughout the rest of their lives. Something would engross every listener in hearing them tell the episode. A part was too personal to share. Neither of them would want to tell anyone their emotions. It was an event common to couples throughout the millennia. They had fallen in love. It's a profound statement known by many. A person blind from birth and miraculously given sight cannot explain how the sight of their first rainbow feels. A person who lived without love cannot explain what he feels even when he knows what he feels is love. The knowledge of such a thing is inborn. The experience is an event in time, waiting to happen, planned long ago, long before the event.

After finishing their meal, together they made a crude attempt at cleaning the kitchen. After a few gestures, they decided that was enough for the evening. The rest could wait for a better day.

"We both need rest now more than anything," Geoffrey stated.

"I agree," the woman answered. "But I don't think the couch is a suitable place for you anymore. The bed's the proper place. I just want to know you're beside me." She looked at him with a simple expression of peace. There was no alluring articulation on her face.

Geoffrey understood. This wasn't a sensual gesture. It was a basic show of the appeal that was clear to the man and the woman. It gave him a sense of self-worth that was strong. She was continually validating this new appraisal he had of himself. He'd found something with her he'd never felt. She wanted to give her heart, the very essence of who she was, over to him. And give it freely. He always had to take anything in his past. No one ever gave anything to him. Any exception came with a price. As he was looking at her, a hermetic peace of mind came over him. He didn't understand it. He reveled in the way it made him feel.

"Thank you, Alex. I know I'll sleep even better with you beside me. I can think of no better way to start tomorrow, waking up together."

Taking his hand, they walked into the bedroom. They quietly prepared for sleep. Laying side by side, they looked into the eyes of the other. The pleasure of that simple gesture was beyond any they had experienced. The joy of the awareness of the other beside them numbed their pain. She reached out her hand and gently caressed his face. He leaned toward her and kissed her on the lips. They closed their eyes and were asleep.

Alex awoke the next morning to hear Geoffrey's utterance of pain. She turned to see him lying beside her. He grimaced his face. "Are you okay?" she asked. There was a note of concern in her voice.

"No," he answered slowly. "I've tried to get up, but I keep feeling a sharp pain in my chest. Lying still during the night, I could breathe with minor discomfort. I'll need your help today. Now I need to lie still for another moment."

"You obviously bruised a rib or two. They will need rest to heal. I'll go fix us coffee. Would you like to sit up a little?"

"Yes."

She held his head forward as she slid her pillow on top of his. "Can you slide up?"

With a moan and some effort, he could sit somewhat upright. "This is as far as I'm going right now!"

"I wish I could make the hurt go away. I guess I'll just have to wait on you hand and foot today. The time you're healed, you poor thing, I'll have spoiled you rotten!" she said with a big grin on her face.

Trying not to smile too much, he said, "Alex, please don't make me laugh. It only makes me hurt." He grinned at her anyway.

"Well, I can see you won't be any fun!" Walking toward the kitchen, she turned in the doorway to look at him. "You stay right there, okay?" She winked at him and went into the kitchen. He laughed a little, moaned, and smiled.

This was an unfamiliar experience. Finding joy in the simple pleasure of each other's company. The bantering and joking felt refreshing to two souls so unaccustomed to it. It was as if something in the air made them feel good being alive. The source was neither the air nor anything else in this world. It flowed from a provenience beyond their understanding. At the moment, they didn't want to infer anything. They only wanted to experience. They only wanted to experience each other. Love does that to two special people.

Alex returned with coffee and toast. The couple sat together in bed, enjoying the totality of this simple event. The conversation was minimal but poignant. Time had slowed to a crawl. The day seemed to last forever. The following days proceeded the same. They each were slowly healing from what the mountain inflicted on them. Geoffrey could move with little pain. Alex didn't appear a mess anymore. Their private world created good feelings. They each knew it had to change.

12

They were sitting on the deck enjoying their coffee flavored with salt air and sunshine. Alex spoke. "Iosefa will return any day now. We have to make plans. You can't stay here in anonymity forever. I've an idea. I should have a boat. I no longer want to be trapped on an island. I'd like the ability to go to the main island. We need to get you off this island. I assume, since you said you were going to Samoa, your new identity papers are there. When he arrives, I'll ride back with him. I'll explain what I want to do. I'll let him keep supplying me as he has in the past. It serves me well. I don't have to deal with it, and I know he needs the money. After all he's done for me, I wouldn't want to stop that. I'll buy a small cabin cruiser and return here. One night we can go to where you have you documents. Once you have them, we can get rooms in the same hotel. There we'll meet and become good friends. I'll introduce you to Iosefa and a few people I know. You and I will come back to the island together. No one will give it a second thought. What do you think?"

"Alex, I once said to myself after one of your early lectures to me, 'that's one smart cookie.' You sized up our situation well and read my mind. I'll have to always remember that about you. I have papers in a safe deposit box in Apia on Upolu. There's a Canadian passport, birth certificate, citizenship card, and Canadian permanent resident card. I know this doesn't surprise you. All it takes is money. I've always liked my first name. Don't ask me why. I thought it best not to change it. If I took a new name, I may forget one day when someone addressed me. It could cause questions to be asked. My new name is Geoffrey Campbell."

"We're going to be a good team, Mr. Campbell. You and I think alike. We'll have to watch for Iosefa's boat. He always comes early in the day. When he comes, you'll have to hide in the storage shed behind the cabin. He brings my supplies up here. While we're putting them away, I'll explain my plan to ride back with him and buy a boat. I'll have a bag packed so I can stay a couple of days if necessary. We'll leave at once. You'll have the place to yourself. Don't sit around in your shorts all day eating chips and drinking my wine!"

He laughed out loud. It felt good to laugh without pain. "Yes, ma'am!"

Iosefa arrived the next morning, and they started their plan. All went according to their preparations. As soon as Geoffrey could see the boat enter the open waters of the Pacific, he went back into the house to await Alex's return.

Riding back to the main island together, Iosefa thought he knew Alex well. She had appeared a lonely, sometimes depressed individual. He felt it was best for both of them to keep his distance. They had shared conversations. He knew her mind was always somewhere else. During most of his visits, he felt pity for her. He knew nothing about her past. Discussing it may only worsen her outlook if he asked questions she didn't want to answer. He was always polite. He treated her as his employer, which she was. But today was unmistakably different. He noticed it as soon as he walked into her cabin. Her face shone with the radiance of the sun. She walked as a gazelle bounds across the savanna. Her voice had the soft sweetness of a wood thrush. Her words drew him in. He sensed a new Alex with a new attitude. Once they were in the boat, Alex continued talking to Iosefa. She seemed to find a pleasure in it. It now wasn't like previous conversations. After proceeding on their course for a few minutes, Alex paused from her discourse. Iosefa spoke.

"Alex, we've become good friends since I first brought you here. You were not a cheerful person then. I've watched you in the many meetings I've had bringing you supplies and the trips going back to

Apia. You slowly came out of the shell you were living in when you arrived. You often spoke of the pleasures you'd found living on your island. It pleases me to see you welcoming life again. I never discussed it with you. Your past life is your business. But today, you're a disparate person. It goes beyond happy. You have a glow on your face and your spirit appears uplifted. You seem to have found joy. Joy can only come from knowing God. Did you have a spiritual revelation since my last visit?"

The statement hit Alex like none in her life before this moment. It took her breath away. Alex had been the one in control. She prepared for the unexpected, always knowing what to say. All these attributes vanished like a wisp of smoke in the wind. Formerly towering psychologically over her adversaries, she now felt diminutive. Iosefa transcended all she had thought of herself.

A look of consternation was on her face. "What did you say?"

"You're different, Alex. Something happened to you since I last saw you. It's what I see in you."

Alex wasn't sure how to ask the next question. She didn't know if she should. Like the Alex of old, she wanted answers. She just came out with it. "Are you a Christian?"

"Yes," he answered. "A Christian family raised me. My parents taught their children about Jesus. We read the Bible daily. We're in church studying the Word every Sunday. You seem surprised. Did you think only Americans are Christians? Missionaries first came here in the 1830s."

The air once again left her lungs. She drew a breath and spoke. "I've never thought about this. My parents never went to church or discussed such matters. I don't know what their beliefs were besides money and power. I know my life has been far from what you speak of. I don't know how to respond."

"Okay. Let's start with your new attitude. You're a new person, Alex. Tell me what happened."

Suddenly, Alex felt as her counterparts must have felt at her acquisition meetings—helpless and speechless. She knew she'd have to tell him something. She thought about how she felt. This would be the discussion without mentioning Geoffrey.

"Iosefa, something happened to me. I found something that had eluded me. I discovered a purpose and meaning in my life. Now I think about giving and not taking, loving and not hating. Looking toward the future and not the past, I guess I washed my past away. I feel clean and ready for what lies ahead. Does it show that much?"

"Yes, it shows. And what I see, you cannot learn from a book. You don't wake up one day with this new awareness of life. Something spoke to your heart, Alex. Only God can do that."

Breathe, Alex, breathe, she thought to herself. "But I don't know God."

"Maybe so, but he knows you. He always has."

Alex's mind was spinning like a top. She grasped for a hold of what was happening but couldn't. Her thoughts were beyond her control. She'd have to ask Iosefa something she'd never asked of anyone. She'd have to ask him to explain this to her.

"Iosefa, you'll have to explain what you're talking about. You obviously know about this." Another change had come over Alex again. A naive ignorance of something very profound had manifested itself in her life. She couldn't let it go by saying she wasn't interested. He knew something she did not. She wanted to know.

They spent the rest of the trip to the Apia in a one-sided conversation. Iosefa talked and Alex listened. What someone else was saying enveloped her. This was a new subject, and she was soaking up every syllable. One cannot get the totality of the Word on one boat ride. She'd experienced so many emotions, so much change over the past days. It was as if all the reasons and answers to her thoughts were coming from the mouth of her friend. She knew there was truth in his words. It was as if he had introduced her to a new language. With only a brief conversation, she felt like she understood this new language.

As they approached the harbor, Iosefa changed the conversation. "Alex, I'd love to continue talking to you. The wonders of God's love and what his love can do for you are limitless. I want you to come to my house this evening and meet my mother. I've spoken of you often to her. She'd be proud to have you in her house. You can have dinner with us. I owe you after all the times you fed me. My mother would want to continue our discussion. I know a man who has a boat for sale. It's what you need. He's a friend, and he'll give you a fair price. We'll call him this evening, and I'll take you there in the morning. I'll take you to the hotel. You can take a taxi to our house this evening. I'll give you the address. Would five o'clock be okay?"

"Yes, that'd be fine." Alex just wanted off the roller coaster she was on. Feeling overwhelmed, she couldn't wait to get to the hotel and lie down. She'd never felt this sensation until now.

13

Alex arrived at Iosefa's house promptly at 5:00 p.m. Iosefa met her at the door, and she entered the small frame house. The humble yet functional furniture and the scattered pictures, blended with the simple decor in the room and spoke of the heart of this house. They spoke not to themselves but to those who entered. Alex heard what they spoke. There was love everywhere within these walls. She found a stately woman sitting in a chair in the corner. Two young girls were playing on the floor.

Iosefa introduced them. "Mother, this is Alex. Alex, my mother, Filemu."

Alex walked over to the woman. She took her outstretched hand in hers and gave it a gentle squeeze. "I'm so pleased to meet you. I guess it's sad that Iosefa and I never discussed our separate lives."

The kindly woman spoke in response. "Well, dear, we can't do anything about the past. And it does not promise the future. We only have today. Today, you are here with us. It pleases me. My son has spoken of you often. I hope your world can be brighter because of our home. I welcome you to it. Please sit by me on the sofa."

Alex had spent her career making many she came in contact with feel uneasy. This woman beside her now was having the opposite effect. Alex had never felt so welcome.

"You're very kind, Filemu. I know now it was my loss that I've not met you sooner."

"All things happen according to God's plan. He didn't want us to meet until now. But now you are here. We will enjoy the gift of each other's company today. You're a beautiful woman. I sense you have a heart to match. What brought you to our island?"

"It's a long, sad story. I don't think such a story would be proper in your presence. There is no sadness on your face. I'll just say I'm here now and have found what I sought upon my arrival."

"My son told me about your talk and his thoughts during the boat ride here. I'm so happy for you. God always blesses us when we least expect it. He's blessed our family many times. My husband will be home from work soon. We'll have dinner then. Son, take the girls into the bedroom. I would like to talk to this woman."

"Alex, I'll call my friend with the boat and tell him we'll meet him in the morning," Iosefa said as he went to the bedroom with the children.

The matriarch spoke to her new friend about her family. Her husband, three children, and six grandchildren were obviously her world. Intermittently, she praised God as she spoke. She then began speaking to Alex about Jesus as if they had had this conversation hundreds of times. Alex was in a new world and loved every minute. An hour ago, this woman speaking was unknown to her. Alex felt she was in the presence of a dear grandmother. Filemu spoke to Alex as a loving family member. Alex was understanding. She wasn't being treated as a guest in this home. This family treated everyone equally. A profound awareness came over Alex. She realized why they were the way they were. They had love in their hearts. Not just love for someone special. It was love for everyone! She also realized why. They knew something she did not. And it had to do with God. She was hanging on every word Filemu spoke. She wanted to know what they knew.

Iosefa returned to the main room after making his phone call. He sat on the sofa alongside Alex. Shortly thereafter, Iosefa's father walked into the room. He rose to greet his father. "Alex, this is my father, Iakopo. Father, my friend, Alex."

Walking with an air of dignity, the man made his solemn way toward his house guest. Alex rose to meet him. He ceremoniously took her outstretched hand with both of his, gave hers a firm but gentle squeeze, and released them.

"I'm honored to have you in our home. My son has spoken of you. I'm glad the time has come for us to meet. Please have a seat." Iakopo sat in a chair opposite his wife.

He spoke to Alex cordially. Alex sized him up as she did all she met. This time, it was uncommon to what she'd reasoned on previous business encounters during her tenure as a corporate raider. She sensed a regal yet humble man. Compassion enveloped his words. She was now seeing the finer qualities that lie in most people. She had looked for weaknesses in her adversaries. There was nothing weak in these people, not in the way she used to perceive weakness. Each member of this family had a demeanor of unassuming confidence. Unlike her, they had nothing to prove. The ensuing conversations were light and heartfelt. Alex felt great respect for this family.

Iosefa's two sisters and four more children arrived, and the family prepared the dinner table. Alex felt like she was a minor character in a play. She was observing every interaction and listening to each exchange between the family members. She'd never seen such love and closeness between people. A simple fact was plain: she was an equal member of the group. At the end of an enjoyable meal, she felt she'd known these people all her life.

The family returned to the main room after dinner. Adults had their places; the young children played their games on the floor. Alex listened intently as each discussed the events of their day. There was laughter often. Their spirits were high. Joy hung in the room like the flowers on a hyacinth vine in full bloom. The fragrance of their words was perfume to Alex's ears. She'd found a new world with Geoffrey. She'd now found an alternative universe with this family.

The moonlight reflecting off the stained glass hanging in a window told the hour was getting late. Filemu told her daughters it was time to take the little children home.

She spoke to the group. "We all have a busy day tomorrow. I'm sure Alex would like to rest as well. My son will take you to your hotel, dear. We're so glad you came to be with us this evening. You're a sweet lady. I pray you listen to your heart and hear God speaking to you. He wants you with him. Please come again. We can talk more about this."

She reached out to Alex and gave her a loving hug and a kiss on the cheek. "God bless you, child."

Iakopo walked over to Alex and did the same. "God bless you," he said.

For the first time in her life, Alex was at a loss for words. Her heart wanted to speak volumes. She looked at all the loving faces around her and a tear began rolling down her cheek. The thought of parting for the evening created a sadness she did not recognize. She didn't want to leave them although she knew she'd come back.

"Filemu, I can't tell you how much I've enjoyed this evening with you and your family. I've never been a part of a loving family. Please allow me to come back and visit with you. Thank you for your hospitality. Goodbye, everyone."

Iosefa walked toward the door. "Come, I'll take you to your hotel," he said to Alex. Walking toward the door, she turned to look at the family. She knew she'd never forget the room full of smiling, glowing faces.

14

As Iosefa drove, Alex tried to process the events of the afternoon and evening. No longer would she reflect on her past. She saw what an utter waste it had been, not just the remembering but her past life itself. Except for Philip—proud, arrogant, disdainful, insolent people had populated that life. She witnessed the opposite in the people she'd been with tonight. She knew she'd never want to be around people of her past again. The reason was becoming clear. She had changed. Or they had changed her. God had planned the change for her. A light was glowing inside Alex. She'd often been inside herself, trying to understand what it all meant. Why had the events of her life happened? Trying to reason it out for years, she never could. She knew it was a mystery. She'd learned to move past it. Seeing the love in Iosefa's family, she discovered a sagacious explanation of her life. She was realizing her answer lay not in her mind but in her heart. She knew the new people in her life had the answer. They had good hearts. She concluded, *That is where I need to continue to learn. I need to learn to search my heart.* She knew the emotions of her past days with Geoffrey grew out of her heart. The external events were only the stage for her heart's feelings to be acted out.

"Iosefa," she stated, "I've been so wrapped up in myself the last three years. I only discovered the beauty of my island a few days ago. It was always there. I looked but never saw it. I feel the same about you now. What I missed in you! You were only a person bringing me

70

supplies. I never saw the man until now. Another thing I wasted in life. I now see the beautiful things in life. I recognized it in your family. In the past, I would've only analyzed them in my mind. Oh, how I wasted so many encounters with good people. I'm not an evil person. I didn't hang around evil people. There were many good people whose paths crossed mine. Something caught me up in the covetous nature of most people I worked with. We were interested in other commodities besides friends. It involved me in their pursuit of an ever-elusive happiness. One minute we had it. The next minute, it was gone. It was a vicious cycle with no end. I chased what the world chased. No one ever spoke to my heart or from their hearts like your family did tonight."

"No one was trying to impress you, Alex," he answered. "This is the way we live and feel about everyone."

"I know that. I could feel the love in the room. Please ask me to come again."

"I don't have to ask you. You will always be welcome in our home. You can come whenever you would like."

Alex felt overwhelmed again. But this time, it created a sense of pure joy. She was overwhelmed with love, the love she felt in her heart and the love she felt from others.

Love is the most powerful energy in the universe. Love's potential is exceptional and transforming. The true comprehension of their experience of love changes everyone. Books do not hold the words of that discernment. With it, one experiences the fulfillment of life. It's a gift of immeasurable value. But it cannot be bought nor sold. For millennia, people have tried. Each attempt was a failure. Money cannot create the love bond between people. God created it. The weaver who sews this bond knows his craft. He created each stitch using the finest binding material he has. He uses the same fibers of our hearts. Not of the heart pumping the life-giving blood. He uses the fibers he used to weave our souls. The heart of our being. He created this heart with love. We return the love to him by appreciating the care and attention he gives to us. The garment of our essence is a special gift for each individual. Bestow this love on others, and it expands exponentially, ever-increasing in volume and power. This is the cogency of love. Many people seek what they want with a false love. They look in the wrong place. These people always fail. The vigor of true love is eternal. It cannot be extinguished. Once possessed, it's ours forever. Alex was aware of this now. The events of her life since Geoffrey washed up on her beach shone a bright light on this revelation. What she had sought had always been available. She only had to take possession of it. The gift was always hers. She accepted this gift now. Her heart glowed with the light of this gift of love.

In her hotel room, Alex showered and prepared for bed. Eagerly crawling into bed and laying her head on her pillow, she didn't want sleep to overtake her. She wanted to relive the best day of her life. She repeated every word spoken to her over and over in her mind. The picture of the loving, lovable, lavish, living, luxuriant people she had been with tonight replaced the drear, drab, dismal, dark, dingy images in her mind's vault of worthless collections. She discarded those despicable relics like yesterday's garbage.

15

The sunshine of a new dawn in Alex's life broke through the parted drapes of her room and reflected off a mirror onto her face. The heavenly rays enhanced the glow on her face. It awakened her in more ways than one from slumber. The heaven needed not shine on her now. She had an interior glow that shone externally. The best of makeup artists couldn't create what was hers now, naturally. One's heart can paint the best portrait of one's soul on their face when it has the pallet of the Creator at its disposal. Alex had it all now. She knew in her heart she'd found what she had searched for when she came to her island. Islands are bodies of soil in a sea of water. A person in an ocean of despair can be an island. She didn't feel like an island now. She knew he had created her as part of a continent. It was to be explored and lived. She was ready to begin her journey.

The phone rang as she was preparing for the day. "Good morning, Alex," Iosefa said when she answered.

"Good morning to you too," she responded.

"The man I told you had a boat to sell cannot show it to us until this afternoon. His name is Liko. He asked that we meet him at one o'clock. I can use this morning to tend to business. If you'd like, I can pick you up and take you to spend the morning with Filemu. The house is on my way. My sister will be home today and will keep her girls. I know my mother would enjoy your company."

"That'd be wonderful, Iosefa," Alex said.

"I'll be at your hotel in thirty minutes. Can you meet me outside?"

"I'll be waiting. Thank you for what you are doing for me."

"Glad to help. Goodbye."

Alex realized the brightness of the day to her eyes was now matched by the brightness in her heart. She was going to spend the morning with her new friend. That thought hit home. The friendship she'd found with Geoffrey was growing into something far beyond her view of friendship. But the friendship she'd discovered with Filemu was different, wonderfully different. Alex realized she was in school. She was aware of a teacher. This teacher was not as she'd experienced in college. This teacher wasn't teaching her mind; he was teaching her heart. The lesson today was about relationships. She understood the word. Now she was understanding the meaning. Any association with the word *relationship* in her past would've been referring to something casual, temporal. The people who populated her world of the past often heard the word *relationship*. The word never referred to something that lasts. And they did not refer to it with the word *love*.

Alex was going this morning to establish a relationship. It would be known as friendship. Lovers are friends. If not, they are not lovers. But there's a special bond between two women who become friends, good friends. There is a purpose expressed by the love between good friends. There is a commonality of thought. The bond the Creator places between two women is purposeful to his plan. The capacity to give love is greater in women than in men. He placed the nurturing, caring, compassionate love of women in them for this purpose. A man learns the true meaning of love from the woman he loves. He loves but isn't aware of its purpose. To him, it has no purpose. It only pleases him. Love to a woman is to please others. That is the essence of true love. Love is a *gift*. Women are givers of this gift.

Alex was waiting outside the front of her hotel when Iosefa arrived. Upon entering his truck, they exchanged smiles. Alex had to comment on it. "Iosefa, we've met countless times over the years. I can't remember ever smiling at you when we met. I'm so sorry!"

"Don't let it trouble you. I know why. That's in the past. God worked it all out for the best. I trust God. I knew he had a plan for you. I had to be patient and wait to see it. I did yesterday. You only lived the first three years on your island. For the first time, you feel life. I can see the vitality in you. You discovered God before I picked you up and brought you to the mainland. You don't have to explain it to me. It's not for me anyway. He planned your experience for you."

The student sat in silence as Iosefa drove to his mother's house. She knew it wasn't so much what she was being taught. It was the intuitiveness of realizing the answers were always present in her life. It was as if the cloud of her self-centeredness cast a shadow over them and kept them obscured. She now felt that this shadow had left her life. This clarity of mind and purpose had always escaped her.

As Iosefa stopped the truck in front of Filemu's house, he spoke. "I called my mother before picking you up. She's delighted I was bringing you over and is eager to spend a few hours with you. She said what a blessing you are to her and awaits your company."

Alex had to force herself to speak. "She thinks I'm a blessing to her?"

"She found great joy in you. Go. You two women have a good morning. I've business to tend to. I'll try to be back here about 12:30."

"Thank you." Alex could think of nothing more to say. Nothing more needed to be said.

Alex knocked on the front door. A joyful "Come in, Alex," sounded from inside. Alex opened the door and entered her alternative universe.

Iosefa returned a little after noon. Upon entering the house, he found joy in the room. The two women were not even aware he had entered. He stood just inside the closed front door, observing. He knew the song well. Filemu was singing to Alex. He'd heard this song many times in his childhood and often when his nieces stayed the night with their grandmother.

> Wake up, my child. Wake up.
> Your face is so mild. Wake up.
> A new day is yours. Come, come see.

It's yours to have. Let it be.
Wake up, my love. Wake up.
Life is there. It's for you to share.
The joy of God awaits.
Come, come see.
It's now your turn. I'll walk with thee.
I love you so. I pray for the best.
I wish you well this day.

Filemu finished and spoke to Alex. "I often sing that to my grandchildren in the morning, when they sleep here for the night. When I go into their room before they sleep, I sing this to them."

Before I rest, sleep, my child.
Dream my child.
Angels watch as you sleep.
God is with you now. You're in his keep.

The woman stopped. Alex looked at her with a new joyfulness in her heart. Their friendship was complete. Silence overtook the room as the occupants reflected on the moment. It was beauty beyond compare.

Filemu spoke first. "Alex, that's a family tradition. My mother sang it to my children. My grandmother sang it to me. It's something the women in our family pass on to the next generation of women."

Alex said, "I had a grandmother when I was very young. I think I last saw her as a child of four years. I remember now what a wonderful person she was. She sang a song to me at night. Then she died, and I guess her memory died as well. Or the new, useless occurrences that were to occupy my life for the next many years pushed it aside."

Filemu noticed her son standing by the door. "Come in, son. We've had a full morning. We talked about many things. Alex understands our Lord. She is on her journey with him now." Then she spoke to her friend. "Remember, dear. God is love. You only need to have faith and trust. With those, God's love will be with you always.

I know you and my son need to leave. Come see me again. I'd like that."

"Filemu, I'll come as often as I can. I've never had a friend like you. Thank you for this morning. It's a morning I'll never forget." She walked to Filemu and gave her an affectionate hug and a kiss on her cheek.

Turning to Iosefa, she asked, "Are we ready to leave?"

"Yes," he answered.

"Goodbye, Filemu," Alex said.

"Goodbye, dear," Filemu answered.

16

They proceeded to the small harbor where Iosefa moored his boat. Liko moored his boat there also, and Iosefa pulled beside it. The two got out of the truck and walked to his friend's boat. They found him inside. They exchanged greetings, and Iosefa introduced the buyer to the seller. Iosefa spoke to Alex. "This is the size you need. It has storage space for your supplies. The large cabin provides cover in bad weather and accommodations in fair weather. Liko and I have discussed the price. His asking price is more than fair. Although the boat is old, he's kept it well maintained. I've been out with him many times on it. I wouldn't let you buy a boat I didn't know you could depend on in the open water."

"I trust you, Iosefa. Tell me how much. We can go to my bank. I can put up stock for collateral. They'll advance me the funds, and we can sign the papers. I'm sure either of you can give me the name of an insurance agent for me to insure it. I want to take the title to the state office and file the transfer. I'd like to get that taken care of today." This was the Alex of old; she took charge. The two men had the same thought. *This woman knows how to do business.*

"I have the title with me," Liko said. "I'll follow you two to your bank."

With the funds and stock Alex had in her account and safe deposit box, the bank advanced her the cash to pay Liko until she could liquidate some assets in a few days. After a simple short-term loan was prepared, Liko had his cash, and Alex had her boat. She and Iosefa went to his insurance agent to have a policy prepared. They went and filed the title transfer. They then drove back to her boat.

"We still have a couple of hours of daylight left. Let's take your boat out. I need to show you everything about owning and using a boat." Alex agreed. She was eager to learn. He gave her lessons on the boat and explained everything from stem to stern. They then went to sea. Alex steered, and Iosefa taught. It was a grand afternoon for Alex. They returned to the harbor. Iosefa took her to see a contractor about building her a small pier on her island to secure her boat to. He agreed to ride over with Iosefa in a couple of days to check it out.

"I want you to stay in your hotel tonight," he said to her. "You'll get more lessons in the morning. You can take it out around the northern shore toward Nu'ulopa. I want you to learn to get to your island. Then we'll return to the dock. I'll only be observing."

"Thanks, Iosefa. You're being more than helpful."

"I want to, and I have to. My mother would skin me alive if I let anything happen to you. Besides, you're part of the family now."

"Thanks. That's the nicest thing anyone said to me. I am a little tired. It's been a wonderful day. I want a good night's rest. I want to reflect on my morning with Filemu."

Back in her room, she eagerly awaited the new dawn. It would be more than she imagined!

Iosefa picked her up at 8:00 a.m. as planned. They proceeded to the harbor. Alex took control of the boat. She drove around the western part of Upolu until she could see the island of Manono. Her island lay just to the west of it. She knew how to get there. She turned and headed back to the harbor when Iosefa spoke.

"I forgot to mention something. It's nothing of importance to you. I read a report from the Samoan police. A fisherman saw a part of a boat about twenty miles south of Upolu. They sent a patrol boat out to investigate. There was a boat hull bobbing in the water. It had burned. The ID numbers were visible on the bow. Searching the surrounding waters, they found no evidence of survivors or bodies. They towed it back and checked the registration with surrounding islands. They found someone had reported it stolen from Fiji. The son of the owner reported it missing. He said his father's financial advisor has asked to borrow it. He told his father it was not a good idea to loan his boat to anyone. Later, he noticed the boat was missing. It was reported his father had died suddenly, about the same time. He assumed the man had taken it, with or without his father's permission. The boat was still missing. The police assume the occupant, or occupants, of the boat drowned, or the sharks got them. It's sad. But I guess no one will ever know what happened."

Alex felt the blood draining from her head. Her head was spinning, and she was falling. She wasn't falling off a mountain. She was free-falling through space. There was darkness around her. Her hands reached out; there was no one there. Her legs buckled, and she hit the deck with a thud.

Iosefa stopped the motor and bent over to pick up Alex. He held her head, patted her cheek, and spoke to her. She didn't respond. He picked her up and took her into the cabin and placed her on the bed. Wetting a towel, he gently stroked her forehead and cheeks with it. He called her name.

Alex slowly opened her eyes. Dazed, she asked, "What happened?"

"I don't know. I was talking. I realized you had fainted and fell. Are you feeling okay?"

"I think so. I blacked out for a moment."

"You lie here for a few minutes. I think the last couple of days have been too much for you. So much has happened. I'm going back up and start the motor. I don't want to drift too long. I think I'll head back to the harbor. Will you be okay?"

"Yes, I think so," she said. Iosefa went back to the deck.

No, I'm definitely not okay, she thought to herself. *Geoffrey lied to me. He didn't tell me everything. He stole a boat, and the owner is dead. What's going on? I was lost, then I found love. Then I found a greater love and a loving family. Life was getting better each day. Now it seems God has pulled the rug out from under me. I thought I'd found the answers with what Iosefa and Filemu taught me. They didn't teach me about this. I don't know what to believe. Oh, Alex. Why do you always have to lose what you love? Why can't I find love, and it lasts more than a moment?*

I thought you wanted me, God. Is this the way you treat people that love you? Alex felt so lost, so alone. She wanted to just double up in a ball and cry. *Why? Why? Why can't I find joy in living that lasts? How many times must I lose what I love?* Tears rolled down her cheeks. She had never felt so alone. She felt like an island again.

After a while, she composed herself. She knew she had to deal with this. Wishing wouldn't make it go away. She needed to get back and talk to Geoffrey. She wanted to talk to God. The thoughts of Filemu's words of faith and trust were swirling in her mind. The always in control Alex of old was competing with the new Alex. The new Alex of love and trust. She needed time to think. She went on deck to join Iosefa.

"Are you feeling okay?" he asked as she stepped up onto the deck where he stood steering the boat.

"Yes," she replied. "I'm okay. It's been a long day. I want to go to the hotel. A nice, warm bath and a good night's sleep will help. I'll feel better in the morning."

"That's a good plan. I'll take you there. I'll pick you up in the morning whenever you're ready to leave. I think you will be better tomorrow for the trip."

"Thank you." She could say no more. Words were not at her disposal now. The two drove back in silence.

Upon entering her hotel room, she drew a tub of warm water. Once in, the soothing effects of the bath diluted the thoughts in her mind. She knew the answers she sought to her many questions would not magically appear in her mind. She needed to hear from two people, God and Geoffrey. She knew she'd hear from Geoffrey. She prayed she'd hear from God.

17

The hotel phone ringing woke Alex the next morning. She reached for the phone as she tried to shake the slumber from her mind. "Hello."

"Good morning, Alex." She recognized Iosefa's voice. "How are you feeling today?"

"Better than I did when you dropped me off. I want to go to my island. Can you pick me up?"

"Yes."

"Give me forty-five minutes. I'll meet you out front."

The ride to the boat was quiet. Alex was deep in deliberation. Iosefa now knew his friend well. He left her to her thoughts as he drove. He spoke when they arrived at the dock. "Alex, I have two fishing charters scheduled. I need to prepare my boat. Can we keep this lesson short? I'll keep this to the basic operation of the boat."

"Of course. I can't express how much I appreciate what you've done for me since you brought me here. Meeting your family and getting to know all of you has changed my life. I'll always look forward to your supply trips to my island now."

After thirty minutes, it satisfied Iosefa that Alex could handle the boat by herself. She was a capable woman and an excellent student. They said their goodbyes. Iosefa proceeded along with his daily routine. Alex proceeded into the unknown.

Alex rounded the island of Manono and saw her island. She felt a sense of relief and anguish, joy and sorrow. *I envisioned my trip back differently. I thought it'd be such a joyous occasion.*

She had prayed to God during the trip. It was a one-sided conversation with her. She neither felt nor heard anything from him. *Maybe I'm not doing it right*, she wondered. *This is so new to me.*

As she approached her island, her sense of awareness returned. In the past, she'd only been a passenger. Iosefa had been the captain, and he knew these waters. She realized she did not. There were coral reefs under her. The boat slowed. The coral reefs appeared through the crystal clear water. Parts of it had grown to just beneath the surface of the water. She picked her way, turning this way and that. She maneuvered her way to the shoreline. Looking up, she saw Geoffrey standing on the beach. His broad smile and waving arms wiped away all the thoughts she had on the trip back. Her heart was ecstatic.

As the boat grounded itself in the soft sand, she turned off the motor. Walking around to the bow, she tossed him a rope. He grabbed it and tossed it out on the beach behind him. Running through the shallow water, he reached the place below the deck where she was standing. Holding out his arms, he said, "Come. I'll catch you. I've been waiting for this moment for days!"

A giddiness came over her. She felt like a young girl. Without hesitation, she leaped the few feet into his arms. Catching her, the momentum pushed him backward into the shallow water. Clutching each other, they rolled on their sides. The water was only inches deep. They kissed passionately as a gentle wave washed over them.

The event cleared her memory of all but one thing. She remembered a place. A place with no past. No future. Only the present. It was a place where only she and Geoffrey existed. She left that place a few days ago. She was back there now. Not realizing it, she was not in control. Her emotions had taken over, and they charged ahead. She didn't want the moment to end, and the fervor of it hoped time would stand still.

He stood and helped her up. Hugging her firmly, he looked into her face. "I can't explain how much I missed you."

Alex could hear him talking. It mesmerized her. She didn't realize how much she had missed him. She was longing for the way she felt with him. She went to her happy place. The love she left here returned like a tsunami. It washed over her consciousness, pushing aside all other thoughts that were in its path.

"I walked the beach often, hoping to see you coming back. I wanted to be on the beach waiting for you."

The touch of his skin on hers brought back memories, wonderful memories. The sound of his voice. She recognized it like she had heard it all her life. She didn't want his embrace to end.

"I was a good boy, like you told me. I didn't eat any chips and only drank a couple glasses of wine. I saved an excellent vintage for your return. I think it's last month's."

Once again, she wasn't in control of her thoughts. The ardor of how she felt toward Geoffrey had taken over. The dormant volcano that erupted while she was with him now poured its lava of love over her. It flowed over her like the fire in her heart.

"I love your boat. Did you get a good deal?"

The walks on the beach, watching the sunsets on the porch, the memory of the mountain, the dinners together. These were the memories she'd longed for all her life. She had them now and loved them. She didn't want to lose another love.

"Alex, have you heard a word I said?"

The genuineness of her reality awoke her from the state she was in. Looking up at him, she pulled him toward her. Giving him a loving kiss, she replied, "Every word. You'd have been in big trouble if I found my house littered with empty wine bottles."

The two were gazing at each other. It was another moment frozen in time.

She spoke. "As soon as I arrived in Apia, I bought you new clothes. I didn't want to forget it. I'm sure you tired of wearing my clothes while I was gone. What would your neighbors think of you coming to borrow a cup of sugar? Go in the boat. There's a package on a seat on the deck."

"Thanks. I'm glad you thought of it. Your clothes don't fit me anyway," he said, laughing. He pulled himself up on the boat.

The thought of where she bought the clothes returned. She didn't want to leave this place. *No,* she said to herself. "No!" she shouted out loud.

He turned to look at her. "What did you say?"

"Nothing. Did you find the package?"

"Yes. Here, catch it while I climb down."

Tossing it, he lowered himself to the sand.

"I wanted to have it gift wrapped with a fancy bow. Being the man you are, you wouldn't have noticed. You probably wouldn't have noticed if I'd put in a paper bag."

"You're right. What'd you buy me? I hope you didn't get me plaid shorts and black socks. I don't want to look like a tourist."

"No, I bought you basic island wear. Nothing formal. If we get invited to a black-tie dinner, rent something to wear."

The magnitude of the event was electrifying to the couple. Their jocularity was refreshing. The days apart multiplied the thrill of being with the other. They didn't want to part again. Returning to the cabin, they enjoyed the afternoon. As they sat on the porch that evening, the twosome were lost in expectation.

18

There was darkness over the small cafe in Marseille. They sat at a corner table out of the view of others. The gentle rain tapping on the canopies over the outside tables sang a melody that matched the beat of her heart. She peered through the dark, smoke-filled air and saw his face across from hers. It stirred her. Why had he brought her here? She joined him in this place because of the intrigue. He had spoken of such exotic places. She wanted to go to those places with him. Why? It didn't matter. She was here, now.

"I love the way you do your hair," he said.

She was in his trance. She waited for his next word.

"I've wanted to be with a woman such as you. Your charm is beyond my expectations."

She looked into his dreamy eyes, and her will melted like the wax running down the cheap candle lighting the worn table under it.

"I've never met a man like you," she confessed sheepishly.

"My dear, you are all I've waited for. I hungered for a woman like you. And now you are mine."

She was in his control. She couldn't withstand his advances even if she wanted to. Her heart skipped a beat…

* * *

Then she heard…"Alex, I've been thinking." Geoffrey's face looked serious.

Shaking her head, she asked, "What were you thinking?"

"Now that we have a boat, we need to go ahead with our plan. I think we should go to Apia, and I can get my new identity. We can stay a few nights in a hotel like we planned. I can buy a plane ticket and leave in a few days to take care of my money."

Alex felt as if someone had hit her in the stomach with a sledgehammer. She was aware of cracks forming in her heart and knew it was about to break. She had a problem, and she'd have to deal with it. The Alex of old reappeared, and she hated it. *I always have to deal with problems. When will they end?*

Alex spoke. "Too much happened while I was gone. I don't know where to begin. Being with you again made me happy. I put it behind me. But we need to talk now."

Geoffrey knew his sweetheart well. He'd seen this part of her when he first encountered her. For whatever reason, she wanted to say something important. He knew it'd be about them. He waited for her to begin.

"During my ride back with Iosefa, he noticed the change in my attitude. He saw what love does to a person. For the first time since I met him, I was happy. No, joyful. I was bubbling over with conversation. My demeanor was different from our previous boat rides together. He said he knew something had happened to me since his last visit. He asked me if I'd had a religious experience. The question shocked me. I told him I didn't know what he was talking about. But I knew I'd have to explain my new disposition. I told him I'd found a purpose and meaning in my way of life. I now thought about loving. Now I thought about the future. I told him I was ready for what lay ahead for me. I couldn't tell him about you, only my feelings that have grown in me since you became part of my life. He said something had spoken to my heart, and only God can do that.

"I now believe he was right on both points, Geoffrey. The love I feel for you is beyond anything I was aware someone could feel. I've felt it grow in me hour by hour since bringing you to my cabin. Why a stranger would stir this in me has puzzled me. I sensed there was a greater force at work beyond what my mind could comprehend. I think you felt the same. I can't call it God or anything else at the moment. This was all so new to me. But it was to change once I got to Apia. I asked Iosefa if he was a Christian. He said yes. He talked to me about Jesus and God on the way back. Geoffrey, it answered all my questions in life. It's hard for me to put into words. He took me to his house to meet his family. Oh, Geoffrey, I've never met such a loving, caring family. They spoke to me and treated me as one of the family. I found I was a part of a family. It's a family of believers in God. I had never associated with people like them. It was a joy to be with them and to know them. The time in Apia was an incredible awakening to me. I want to talk to you about it. I want you to learn to be part of this family of Christian people. We both have much to learn, and I want us to learn it together. I want us to get married. I want a new life. A new life with you."

Geoffrey could only stare at Alex like a deer in the headlights. It froze his body and mind. It seemed he was incapable of thinking. "Alex, you need to slow down. This is way too much for me. We had a great thing together. I thought it was even better since you came back. Now you're a different person. And marriage, why is it necessary?"

"No, Geoffrey, I'm not a different person. I'm the same person with the same feeling toward you. I came back as a complete person. I found what I sensed was missing. I found it with Iosefa's family. The love I found and feel for you is different. There is more than one love in this world. We saw that in our previous lives. All the loves people thought they had were only self-created mirages. The love we have is real. The love I found with his family is real. We aren't who we think we are. We are who God created us to be. Everyone aspires to one or the other. I want you to have an open mind. I did. I can explain it to you. Geoffrey, this is very important. It's more than what we have now."

"Alex, we had something great before you left. It was beyond my wildest dreams. Now you want to squash it for something else. I can't see what you want. It's a genuine tragedy. It's tragic what you want to happen to our relationship."

"No, Geoffrey, the genuine tragedy of a person is when he's afraid of the light. Maybe I have sprung this on you too fast. I'm sorry. We waited our entire life for what we have now. You must understand there's a greater force at work than our human emotions. I know you'll see this when we talk more. I've no calendar on this island. Let's not rush into anything. A man and a woman must be able to talk to each other about difficult subjects, keeping an open mind toward the feelings of the other. Without that, their love will not last. It cannot withstand the storms of life." She leaned over and kissed him gently. "I love you more than I can tell you. I only want what is best for us."

Her eyes peering into his waved a magic wand in his mind, and all previous thoughts vanished. "I love you too, Alex. I've been walking on air since you came back. I suddenly felt the ground under me. Let's not spoil your return. I've thought of a special dinner for you. I went out and speared two Samoan crabs. I want to treat you to a wonderful meal. I reserved a special table for you. Plumeria and frangipani flowers adorn it. I went through your wine collection and picked out the best. I know the vintage will be superb in your company. Let's enjoy this evening and not discuss any other matters, okay?"

"Geoffrey, every moment with you is special. I want tonight to be even more." She knew there was much more to talk about. She was as caught up in the intensity with him. She wanted this to be an exceptional night as much as he did. The duo prepared a celebratory banquet. It was an enchanting night.

19

The first light of morning peeking over the line where the ocean met the sky stirred Alex from her troubled sleep. She had not rested well. The enchanting evening with Geoffrey was more than she expected. She didn't want the memory of it to leave. This one she stored on a shelf to be recalled and relived. The dawn of a new day was the dawn of a new reality. She had to face it. She looked over at Geoffrey, still deep in sleep. Her love welled up inside of her, and she thought it'd take her breath away. *No,* she said to herself. *"I have a problem, and I must deal with it.* She knew ignoring it'd only postpone to another day the pain she'd experience. I can't find a solution to this problem even though I'm good at dealing with them. She rose from the bed and put on a robe. After getting ready, she went into the other room. She needed time to think. She prepared a pot of coffee, poured a cup, and went out onto the porch.

There was beauty everywhere. The gentle waves rolling softly over the brightly colored coral beneath them created a kaleidoscope of ever-changing colors. Shimmering hues of the greenish-blue water gave life to a constantly changing palette that the Creator chose for this scene. The infinite shades of green adorning the foliage on either side were vivid against the background of the soft-blue sky. The animal life in the sky and in the water made it known God was present today. Alex saw none of it. Her gaze was inward. Her thoughts blocked out the beauty everywhere, even in her heart, for the moment.

She prepared in her mind what she'd say. She had been known for making her adversaries aware of where she stood and what she intended to do. She had been determined to win and for them to lose. She'd plotted her strategy and then executed it. In the past, she used this method to succeed. She wanted that to not happen today.

She didn't want to win. If she won, she could lose everything. This situation had to be approached differently. *What am I to do?* She knew she could not keep silent about what Iosefa had told her. People in love cannot hide secrets from each other. Secrets are like a hot ember, simmering, never to be extinguished. Coming in contact with some tinder would start a blaze that would consume those around it. Secrets will kill any relationship. Somehow, Alex knew this. Keeping silent was not a choice. Neither could she be confrontational. A relationship cannot be equal if one feels he is better than the other. She knew she could not accuse Geoffrey of anything. She had no direct knowledge. The circumstantial evidence she knew and what she inferred from Iosefa told her there was more to learn. No, it was what she must learn. They were going to discuss their lives and feelings with each other.

The totality of the situation was suddenly vivid in her mind. A week ago, she was alone on her island, seemingly at peace with herself. A walk on the beach, an encounter never experienced, a mountain, a boat ride to the main island, God now present in her life, a new genuine friend in Filemu, and now here on the porch this morning. A week in Alex's life. A lifetime to many.

God, she said to herself, *please, help me. I don't know what to say or do. Please tell me how I am to handle this. This is so new to me. God, you are so new to me. Filemu told me I must trust you. I have no choice and no answer. I trust you will make the answer known to me. You know I love Geoffrey. God, I don't know if I could take losing another love. How many times? Hasn't it been enough?*

She waited and didn't know what to expect. She wished something would speak to her. Alone with her thoughts, she knew what she needed most was the strength to deal with her problem. Emotions are not strength. If so, she could replace Atlas in holding up the world. She didn't know why that thought came to her. Her mind was spinning. She wanted it to stop so she could clear her mind. She couldn't. Her feminine emotions were at a fever pitch now. She closed her eyes. She needed to think. She couldn't. She could only dream once again.

* * *

After the family meal, her father had told her he wanted to talk to her. She followed him to the parlor. He closed the door after she had entered. "Sit down, Alexandria," he said. His voice had a stern tone to it. "Alexandria, I've spoken to you before about my feeling for this boy you've been seeing. You continue to see him without my permission. I know of these things. I have my reservations." Her father spoke with the authority of the man of the house. In those days, there was only one authority, the father. The man of the house. People in those days understood and accepted this. It was as life was then. "I've heard things about him, and I cannot condone you seeing him. I would ask that you reconsider your feelings for him. I think you are being too emotional. There are many fine, suitable men for you to marry. Your mother has spoken to me of them. She has met most of them and approves of them. We know what is best for you."

A tear of sorrow formed in her eye. She knew it didn't matter what she said or what she felt. His decision would be final. A young, proper woman didn't do otherwise.

"Father, I know he has his faults. But I don't want to marry a man I don't love. I love the one I want."

"Nonsense. Your mother and I were not in love when we married. We learned what it was. We turned out to be a respectable couple. We only want the same for you and your sisters."

She felt trapped. She felt trapped between love and losing that love. It was not hers to decide. Other circumstances would decide the outcome. The unsparing look of her father told she'd have to obey him.

"I consider this matter closed. You need to forget this person. You need to do what is right."

She didn't know one's heart could feel such sadness.

* * *

"Can I join you?" she heard behind her. Geoffrey was in the doorway with a cup of coffee. The smile on his face and the gleam in his eye renewed her joy. Her heart overcame that which she had in her mind a moment ago.

Setting his cup down, he reached down to her and pulled her up from her chair. Holding her against his chest, he kissed her passionately. Alex was not home at the moment. She was in different places, different dimensions. The love she had for this man, whether he was right for her or not, consumed her.

He peered deeply into her eyes, and he felt the beauty he beheld draw her into the depths of his soul. It was as if he wasn't standing before her. She was now part of him. He perceived they had become of one spirit. His mind was now one with hers. Intertwined, he sensed he couldn't free himself from her if ordered to do so.

Alex looked at his face. She had always been in control. Her self-control was her foundation. This foundation was suddenly in the throes of a violent earthquake. It shattered as a glass falling to a hard surface. All she tried to keep deep inside of her came pouring out. She sobbed. Then she was crying uncontrollably. Tears of such sorrow never felt before were streaming down her cheeks. She pulled away from him and sat down. She put her face into her hands.

Geoffrey didn't know what to say at the moment. It was a moment that many men experience. He knew he was with a woman. He sat beside her and put his hand on her arm. Knowing her, he understood there was something terribly wrong. He felt it had to do with her talk to him about God and marriage yesterday. He waited.

Alex composed herself. "Geoffrey, I love you so much. I wish I didn't have to ask you the questions I must ask. We must know everything about each other to have a life together. I know you love me. I know you have a heart of love. But I need to know what else is in that heart.

"After I bought the boat, Iosefa took me out to teach me everything about how it works and how to use it. On the way back to the harbor, he told me a troubling story. Over a week ago, a fisherman saw a burned-out hull of a boat bobbing in the water twenty miles south of here. The Samoan police went out to investigate. They found no survivors or bodies. They took it back to Upolu. When they checked the registration numbers with the surrounding islands, someone had reported the boat stolen from Fiji. He said the son of the owner reported it because his father had just died suddenly. The son said his father's financial advisor had asked to use it. After the boat had been gone too long, he reported it to the authorities.

"You didn't tell me you stole a boat, Geoffrey! An omission of relative facts is a lie to me. The owner died at the same time. Did you cause his death? Oh, Geoffrey, I thought I trusted you. Now I don't know what to believe. I don't know if I want to hear what you have to say. I don't know if I can believe anything anymore."

The sadness in her face broke Geoffrey's heart. He realized something perceptive. It hurt him she could think he could cause her sorrow. He knew he couldn't do it deliberately. A sense of sadness came over him. Could he cause such in her? He also felt something that created an equal sadness in himself. It was like she was slipping away. He wouldn't allow that to happen.

20

Geoffrey knelt in front of her. With his hand, he gently wiped the tears from her cheeks. Taking her hands in his, he said, "Look at me, Alex."

Through tear-clouded eyes, she looked at him. It terrified her. She so feared that he'd say something that'd forever destroy their relationship. It could never be what it was. She felt she was on the verge of losing another love. Her lips trembled.

"Alex, I can explain. No excuses. No lies. I'm speaking from my heart, Alex. A heart that loves you more than I can say. I wouldn't want to have you because of a lie. You will know what happened.

"First, I didn't steal the boat. The owner, the old man, told me I could use it. He had let me use it once before. His son had come to live with him recently. The man was old and not doing well. I had more money than I needed. It was time to leave. I wanted to leave so that no one could trace my whereabouts. I couldn't take a plane. I knew I could get from Fiji to Samoa in a boat without being noticed. With my new identity, I also have what I'd need to disguise my appearance. Surveillance cameras wouldn't show me. I'd planned to leave the boat in the harbor and send him a wire, telling him where it was. When the authorities put it all together, I'd have changed planes multiple times. I'd have vanished without a trace. Alex, I do not know why he died. I guess old age. I had no reason to cause him any harm. To draw attention to him would have destroyed my plan. I thought the boat was at the bottom of the Pacific. It never occurred to me to go into this entire story. Either way, I'm here now. Alex, you're a smart woman. You can see I had this planned out to the last detail. Except the boat catching on fire and the remains being discovered. Think about this, Alex. I'd have to be stupid to cause that old man any harm and steal his boat. Upon my arrival in Samoa, an army of police would have been all over me." He waited for a response from her.

She looked at him, and it lifted a great sorrow from her heart. There was one thing she knew for certain about him. He was as crafty as she had been. She believed him because she wanted to. She also believed him because she knew it was the truth. She smiled. A bright, glowing smile. She wondered how she could have thought otherwise. It was because she had learned to expect the unexpected in her job. She'd have to discard that idea with the other talents she used. She never wanted to experience those feelings again.

"Alex, this is even better than I had planned. My plan was to vanish without a trace. I knew once everyone realized I had left abruptly; the firm would have audited my accounts. They'd have found that I had skimmed from my customers' accounts. It'd take a while to find the money. I'd have to go to the Caymans before they traced the money. The money and I would be gone by then. But I would've been forever on a wanted list. But now I'm dead! They will assume I died in the fire or drowned. I can go get half of the money. I'll leave the rest in an account. Any good auditor will eventually find it. They'll think I spent the rest and died before they get to the part they found. It will only confirm that Geoffrey Scott is dead. Case closed."

Alex looked at Geoffrey looking at her. Geoffrey looked at Alex looking at him. All the feelings of the past week welled up in each of their minds. Each said they didn't want to lose this. *I love you*, they were saying silently to each other. They knew they wanted each other more than anything else. They both wanted the other to give something. This was the hard part. This is the hard part of any serious relationship. At some point, they must decide. Someone has to give. A lasting relationship always pivots at this moment. There's a secret to special relationships planned long ago not to be revealed. The pair discovers it. Each has to search their hearts, where the wisdom is, and choose. What is best for us? Not what is best for me. The decision has a profound and lasting impact on the individual and the relationship. They learn that the more one gives to the other, the more one receives. This isn't a concept taught. Maybe just the opposite. But once this lesson is learned, the arduous journey is over. The joy of living together begins. These two students were in class now.

"Geoffrey, I believe you. I really do. I know you wouldn't do anything stupid. I'm sorry I had doubts about you. Please forgive me. But now that your entire episode is in the open, the logical conclusion seems obvious to me. I have enough money to support us for the rest of our lives. Like you said, tracing the money to the account, they'll conclude that you died in the boat fire. We can live happily ever after! I want you to learn of the joy of knowing Jesus. I want you to know about him. The happiness shone on Alex's face! She could hardly contain her joy.

Still kneeling before her, he saw the glow on her face. He didn't want to spoil it, but he had one more thing to tell her. "Alex, I want to spend the rest of my story with you. I'll listen to what you want to tell me. First, I want to get my money."

That sledgehammer just hit Alex in her abdomen again. The glow on her face drained like a sieve held it.

"Alex, I don't want to live off your money. I don't want a woman supporting me. I want to contribute to our relationship. Besides, I worked hard for that money. I lay awake many nights wondering if the next day would be the day they caught me. What I was doing was a cat-and-mouse game. No one can play it forever without getting caught. I played the game better than most. I enjoyed winning. I tried to find new ways to continue to be a winner. The owner of the boat was my best client. He had so many millions he had lost count. I made sure his portfolio performed better than others. He loved to gloat about how successful he was with his investments. He gave me free rein on his account this last year. After I took my share of his profits, I knew I had enough. That's when I put my plan in place. I can't leave that money sitting there. I went through too much to get it."

"Is that what you love, Geoffrey, money? I have what we need. Why do you want more? Can you love despite having no money? Can you do that? Why are you always expecting the future? Why can't you live for today, with me, here, like we are now?"

The fear that Alex tried to keep pushed back in the deep well of her psyche was emerging and casting its dark cloud over her. She could feel her body tremble as she felt powerless to stop it. She didn't know if she could survive its punishing blow to her heart again. Each battle vitiated her resistance. A battle-weary heart can only withstand so much. Although unsubstantiated, the doubt forming about Geoffrey weakened her ability to remove the thought from her mind. *Am I going to lose what I love again?*

"Things come at a price. I want to be one of them. I don't want to lose you. I don't want you to leave. You know whether you love me." Alex knew what she was afraid of. She couldn't tell him. She knew it was wrong. Her fear was in control. It created a terror in her. If he left, he wouldn't return. *Why would he?* she thought. *When he gets his money, he can have anything he wants. If he loved me like he said he does, he wouldn't leave. He might meet another woman there. No one would ever discover his past there. He'd have nothing to fear.* Alex had learned from God. She was now getting a lesson from someone else. Evil was using his best weapons: doubt and fear. When one lets them in control, they lead away from that which is good. Alex didn't know the cause of the problem. Filemu had given her tools. She didn't know how to use them.

Geoffrey realized the Alex who had saved him when he washed up on her beach had changed. But the one reason that stuck out now was her dominative nature had vanished. A meekness replaced it, and it puzzled him. Where her personality once stood tall, she'd taken on a humbleness that seemed reluctant to direct her will upon him. He realized this change had come over her since she returned from Apia, when she had found Jesus. He didn't know how to respond to her.

He leaned forward and pulled her close to him. Rubbing her back, he whispered, "I never want to do anything to hurt you, Alex.

It seems that's what I'm doing now. I'm sorry. You're too emotional, and I don't know what to say. Let's go inside for a while. I just want to sit on the couch holding you."

Inside, on the couch, their coupled embrace was beyond words. They were in another dimension in each other's arms. It was a void, empty of any substance. Only they existed. It's not an uncommon place and frequented by many at a moment such as this. It's a place called love.

21

Neither of them wanted to say the first word. Each knew it may not end well. Each desired something the other did not. How would they reconcile their differences? Compromise had never been a word either of them had used in their previous lives. Giving concessions was an unknown trait. A new life lesson class had begun.

Geoffrey untangled himself from their cuddle. They looked deep into each other's eyes. They didn't know a soul could feel love and heartbreak at the same time. Each knew the next step would hurt one or both of them. Somehow, they knew they had to travel on this path. The paths planned for everyone are not always easy. They are often a path down a mountainside. On that mountain path, we find who we are and what we value most. We cannot learn these lessons on a serene walk on a beach. The writer of our lives knew this. If we are to experience what he planned for us, we have to go down paths that aren't pleasant. It's there we discover a very special trait, trust. It's the keel and rudder of our ship of life that keep us on our course. Without it, we have no value system. Everything is transitory and temporal. Without trust, there's neither a future nor an eternity. Even without a lesson from Iosefa, it was as if Geoffrey knew. Alex had the full lesson from Iosefa and Filemu. But evil saw her as a new weapon against him if they continued their hold on her. Evil worked his way into her mind and there planted the seed of doubt. It was his best weapon. He wanted to watch it grow and break that which he feared, trust.

Geoffrey gathered all the will and determination he could muster. He need not think about his love. It was as if it was consuming him. "Alex," he whispered. His speaking her name fell into her ears with the gentleness of a feather falling onto a pillow. "Before the fire on the boat, I was a different man. I don't know if I know that person. I don't know if I ever knew him. I know the man I am now. He is a far better person in a far better place than I could ever had dreamed. If indeed I ever dreamed. I plotted, planned, prepared, and executed. I never thought of anything in life past that point. Now, with you, I see so far. It's beyond my comprehension. I never knew love. I found it with you, here, on this island. How it came to be, I cannot explain. You seem to understand. You are as much a part of me as my arms and legs. I want nothing to take that away. But you must allow me this one thing. It's important to me. I can't explain it more than that. I want to go get my money. I want to share it and the rest of my time with you. Why is this so hard for you? Why don't you want me to go?"

* * *

Once again in that cold, stone-walled dungeon. The same hourglass was placed on a pedestal in front of her. It forced her to watch as the hourglass of her love turned over once again. Geoffrey was in the glass this time. She watched the grains of the love she felt for him fall through the narrow opening into an emptiness. There was no bottom to this hourglass, only a dark chasm. In a few moments, the grains of love would have drained away again. She could do nothing to stop this. It was a recurring nightmare. It turned the hourglass with a love over and emptied. Over and over, again and again. Oh, how she wanted to smash that dreadful thing! She couldn't touch it. It was beyond her reach. And she could not turn from it. It forced her to watch it. It was her continuing torment, just like Prometheus—her emotions endlessly torn to pieces, rebuilt, and readied to be torn apart again. To her, it was her punishment for the money she took, for the lives she ruined. Alex had become accustomed to this. She feared it but knew she could not stop it. She'd have to endure it once again.

* * *

Alex looked at him with cold, apprehensive, doubting eyes. "If you leave, you won't come back!" Tears of fear ran down her cheeks. She could feel her body trembling. "Geoffrey, I'm so afraid this time. I've lost so many loves. To lose this love, you, would be too much. I would not survive. That's why I can't let you leave me. I'm afraid, Geoffrey. I've never been afraid like this before. Please don't leave me!"

Geoffrey's heart was breaking for many reasons. One stood out more than others. The once strong, commanding, dominating woman whose beach he'd washed up on had changed. Dramatically! She was now an unassertive, submissive, powerless woman. Geoffrey felt he had caused this. He wanted the old Alex back. But he knew he couldn't change what had happened between them. He knew it was love. He found love and understood it. She was losing what she found once again. He had heard her speak of so many lost loves. He was understanding a part of her that was locked deep inside. She had always sought love though she didn't know what it was. It was as if her soul would find it, always thinking she had. Then it was gone, only to be sought again. He somehow knew the only way to reach her was with that which she so feared losing. The bond of love between them was strong. He knew this. He hoped she'd draw on this to sustain her until he returned.

"Alex, reach deep inside of yourself. The answer to your fear is there. I love you. You know that. I won't leave you. I'll go away for a short time. Then I'll return, and we'll be together. Then we'll never part. Please believe me!" There was almost a sense of desperation in his voice.

"Okay, go! Go get your money! I don't care anymore! But know this. No one has ever loved you as I have. As I do. You're like everything I've ever loved. You're going to leave me just like they did. Everybody has a dream. What do you dream? You dream nothing, do you? You don't need me! Go! Go! I feel pity for you. But remember this. You will die somewhere, a lonely man. You will go to your grave, and no one will attend your funeral!"

Geoffrey looked at her with a certainty in his soul. He could not find the words to speak what he felt in his heart. His broken heart could only leave for the moment. Turning to walk away, he turned back. His broken heart spoke with tears down his cheeks. "You're wrong, Alex. I won't be alone. You'll be there. You'll be there because you love me." He turned back and left the room.

An aloneness like nobody had ever felt crept into Alex. She felt naked and cold. The emptiness inside of her was growing. It was replacing all that was in her. Soon, she was only an empty shell.

The morning passed into the afternoon. The afternoon ceded to the evening. The evening faded into the dark of night. No moon illuminated the island. It was even darker in Alex's mind. The two islanders were at an impasse. They had spoken casually to the other since Alex had told Geoffrey to leave to get his money. But the feelings were still strong between the two. It was as if neither wanted to engage in any serious discussion lest the situation worsen. They retired for the night.

It was to be another bright and beautiful day in the South Pacific, except for those on Nu'ulopa. The two knew what was about to happen. Geoffrey didn't want to stop it. Alex knew she was powerless to stop it. She had reconciled herself to defeat. Geoffrey knew that if she reached beyond her fear and showed patience, all would work out. The fact of leaving her troubled him. She needed to find herself. *What if something happened while I'm gone?* This thought was reoccurring in his mind. He knew if his worst fears came to reality, the guilt would haunt him all the rest of his life. He might destroy that which he treasured so much. Fear and doubt hung over the island like a cold fog.

22

Each had a cup of coffee and was sitting on the porch. They were reflecting on the events to come. How could two people in love feel so far apart? Geoffrey knew now he had to leave. Alex had more to learn about love. Alex knew she was defenseless to prevent his leaving. She felt a frailness that had never been a possibility before. She was on a raft in a raging river. It was being tossed back and forth by the current.

Geoffrey finally spoke. "Alex, I can only say two things. I love you with all my heart and soul. I didn't know it was possible to love someone so. I've spoken nothing truer in my life than that statement. You must trust me. Without that, we have little that will last. When we were first getting to know each other, you doubted what I said. That man no longer exists. The man you see before you is the truth. I can only say what I feel. I cannot make you think differently."

He waited for her to react. She only stared at him with a forlornness to her expression. The misery of her torment took her voice away. Evil had worked his way in her will and was winning the battle. The hopelessness he plants in the minds of his prey can be overpowering. When it becomes the dominant emotion, the depression can be severe. Alex was trying to withstand the onslaught. She sat a few feet from Geoffrey, but he knew she was far away.

* * *

This day created an excitement that was more than any child's dreams. But that is the wonder of childhood. The wonder of what each new day will bring. Each day will bring an adventure never experienced. This was the case today as she walked the midway with her hand in her mother's.

She remembered giggling when her mother had helped her put on the new dress bought just for this occasion. She thought it was the prettiest dress she'd ever seen. Her mother had put her hair in curls with bright-colored bows. The shine on her new shoes sparkled in the light. Never in her brief life of eight years had she felt happier. She didn't know how she'd waited for this day. Her mother had spoken to her about the wonders of the county fair weeks earlier. How magical she thought it would be. She had dreamed every night. Now all she'd dreamed was happening right before her eyes. A kaleidoscope of flashing lights, bells clanging, smells of fresh foods, and music coming from the carousel had her spellbound. Her little mind was trying to comprehend it all. It appeared magical!

Everywhere she saw beautiful things for sale. She wanted to have each of them. Her mother had given her a few coins she could spend as she wanted. She hoped it'd be enough to buy some of everything. Every time she wanted to buy something, her mother told her it cost more than she had. It was too expensive, she'd explain. "You can't have everything you want," the little girl remembered her saying.

For now, being here was enough.

Her mother had stopped at a booth selling homemade jams and jellies. She was no longer holding the little girl's hand as she discussed recipes with the seller. The girl saw the doll booth a few feet away and walked over to it. The dolls on display were those of her most treasured desires. There were all types and sizes. But one caught her eye. This was the one she had dreamed of. This is what she felt in her heart she had always sought. Now she and it were together. The sight of it drew her closer. The thought of possessing it was hypnotic. Maybe it could be hers.

The man at the booth walked over to her. "Hello, young lady. Do you like the dolls?"

Without hesitation, she pointed at her dream and asked, "How much is that one?" The man knew it was beyond what she could have.

Just for sport, he asked her, "How much do you have?"

Reaching into her little purse, she pulled out the coins her mother had given her. She opened her hand and showed them to him. The glow on her face was radiant.

He looked at the pittance and started to speak. Then he saw the face of the child looking at the doll. She was looking only at the doll. The joy of the occasion and the moment created a portrait. It shone with the gleam in the eyes, the smile from the lips, the glow in her cheeks. All the love and dreams in her heart were being poured out at the moment. Her little heart had waited and now, in her mind, her dream was to become real. The man knew that when he spoke, he'd break her poor heart. Something outside of himself spoke to him. He said something he never thought he'd say, and not for this reason. "Young lady, that's just enough."

Oh, would her little body be able to contain the thrill that was welling up inside of her! A joy indescribable overwhelms the mind. It cannot comprehend the unimaginable happening in their life.

He took the coins from the small, outstretched hand, replacing them with the doll. He knew if someone paid the price he wanted, it'd have only been more money in his till. Tomorrow it would be part of the insignificance of his past. But the sight of the face of the little girl holding that doll would last him a lifetime.

She clutched it to her chest and felt a love swell up in her. She didn't understand it, but it was real. Turning, she walked to go back to her mother.

After a few steps looking at the doll, she looked up to see her mother. But she did not. She looked around. Still, she didn't see her. I must have turned the wrong way, *she thought. She walked back to the booth and went a few paces in the other direction. Still, she didn't see her mother. She knew she was close. She walked here and there. Her pace quickened, as did the beating of her heart. "Mother," she called out. She walked in circles, calling over and over, "mother." Still no answer.*

All she saw were tall people moving in every direction. No one noticed her. "Mother, mother," she cried as tears ran down her cheeks. The people became taller as she became smaller. Someone bumped her hand as she began running, looking for her mother. She lost her purchase, her precious love. It didn't matter. She felt lost. No one knew her. No one knew where she was. No one knew how she felt. How could anyone know how she felt? Feeling a hand on her shoulder, she heard a voice she knew.

* * *

"Alex, we need to go. The flight I need to be on leaves this evening."

Alex was always in control. Now Alex was out of control. She had an additional problem. She'd lost control of herself. This was not a problem she had ever expected nor dreamed of. And there was no fix for this problem. The problem was controlling her mind. At the moment, she's as scared as a lost little girl. She didn't know what was controlling her.

"I want to catch the next flight to Auckland, New Zealand. Then I can fly direct to Buenos Aires, Argentina. A couple more flights to lose my tracks, and I'll be in the Cayman Islands. I'll then move the money to Swiss bank accounts. I can launder the money through dummy international corporations and then back to a numbered account where it'll be safe. This will take three weeks. Then I'll come back through Canada. I'll just be a Canadian tourist here to see Samoa. We'll be together again."

He took her in his arms and hugged her with all his love. Alex felt this love. She wanted to believe it would last. She looked into his eyes and knew she loved him. She also saw his love for her in those eyes. There was no doubt about the love each felt for the other. She thought of the love of Jesus Filemu taught her. Alex felt a little peace she had not felt lately. A sense of calm came over her. The doubt placed in her was gone for now. She found she could put it aside for a time. Reaching deep inside of herself, she found a tool she still didn't know quite how to use. She was still learning. The love of Jesus that Filemu had taught her created a sense of power in her. Just thinking of him and the evil couldn't be present at the same time.

"I know I can't stop you, Geoffrey. I still don't want you to go, but I know you'd never be the same or forgive me if I stopped you. I'm trying to find the trust I need. I've loved and lost. I trusted, and it disappointed me. I can't change my past life or what I learned from it. Come back to me, Geoffrey. You have to!"

"I will, Alex. Saying it over and over will not make it truer. I'm going to pack a few items to take. I want to appear as any passenger on the plane. I'll buy what I need and more clothes along the way. Credit cards are with my new identity. When we get to the harbor, I'll need to sneak away. I don't want anyone to see us together. Someone may ask you questions. I think you should stay a night or two and see Iosefa's mother. I'd feel better about leaving you alone if you didn't come directly back here. Will you pack what you need for a couple of days? I'll feel a little better if you would."

"You're right, Geoffrey. And I need to talk to Filemu. I'm going to be so alone with you gone. Being with someone I know will help."

The two packed, boarded the boat, and proceeded to Apia.

23

Upon entering the small harbor, Geoffrey looked for other people. A few people were working around the dock. No one was paying any attention to their boat. Alex guided it to an open spot on the pier, and Geoffrey secured it. They prepared their belongings to leave the boat. In the cabin, they sat beside each other. It filled Geoffrey with anticipation. Alex was feeling despair. Neither wanted to leave the other. Geoffrey knew he couldn't linger long. He hugged her and kissed her as passionately as he could. Looking into her eyes, he rubbed her cheek with his hand and stroked his fingers through her hair. He kissed her again.

"I have to go," he said.

"After you leave, I'll go to the airport too. I want to be with you. No one will think of us more than anyone else. Please, I want to see you before you leave."

Geoffrey saw the look on her face; he couldn't say no. "I'll be checking in with Air New Zealand. Go to where the ticket counter is. I'll be wearing a disguise, but you'll know me. We'll meet between there and the security entrance. He kissed her again and left the boat. He walked to the main road to find a cab. Alex waited a while and did the same.

They each arrived at the airport and proceeded as planned. After Geoffrey had purchased his ticket, he saw Alex sitting close by. He acknowledged her and walked over to a waiting area outside the security check-in. Alex walked over and sat beside him. The old Alex was back again.

"I like your beard. It makes you look distinguished. A business suit with it. You thought of everything. As a matter of fact, I think it's an improvement," she said with somewhat of a smile.

Geoffrey suddenly felt a gaiety he'd not felt recently. "That does it. I forbid you from hanging around bearded, distinguished, well-dressed men while I'm away. I have good looks, money, charm, and a way with a certain woman. You may find something in one of them I don't have."

"I wouldn't worry about them. I once fell for a guy wearing wet clothes and a life jacket. I need little to impress me."

They saw a smile on the other's face. Couples for millennia have sat like this. The man was going to war. It didn't matter the reason; the event had happened to others besides Alex. But to her, it was the same. Deep inside of her, she didn't know if her man would return to her. This couple felt like many others before them. The future would wait. Now there was only now. They were with each other, and nothing else existed. Their facial expressions spoke a slight laugh at a past recollection.

They would not remember the words. They would never forget the look on the others' face. The minutes rushed into hours, and then it was time for him to leave. Parting like this is an indescribable heartache.

Neither of them wanted the last kiss, the last embrace, or the last touch of the skin of the other. One of them had to start the end.

"Alex, you need to remember this. When I return, I'll be on a Fiji Airways flight from San Francisco to Apia. Check the schedule for the airlines. Look for a flight three weeks from now. I'll be on that flight. It's time, Alex. I love you, Alex. Alex, I'll be back. I need you. I don't want to live without you, Alex. Alex!" He stopped speaking.

"I love you, Geoffrey," she said, with a river of grief flowing down her cheeks.

He turned and walked away.

She stood in silence as he walked to the security check-in. Once through, he turned and looked at the woman he loved. She looked at him. It was a moment frozen in time. Love creates such moments. He raised his hand to wave but put it down. It wouldn't have said more than he had already. She raised her hand as high as her face. Holding it there for a moment, she lowered it. She watched as he walked along the concourse, away from her, out of her life. With her gazed fixed on that object as it went away, she stood where she was. Alone, and in silence. She didn't know how long she stood there. It seemed an eternity. But it was only the beginning. The waiting had begun. Could she survive? She didn't know.

Walking back to a seating area where she could see his plane, she sat down. She looked at the plane. It appeared so cold and indifferent to how she felt. *How could such a thing hold something so warm and wonderful as my love?*

Alex sat in the waiting area, looking out over the runway. She watched as Geoffrey's plane taxied down the tarmac to the takeoff point. It turned off the taxiway onto the runway. She saw it bolt down the runway. She closed her eyes. *Oh, God, bring him back to me.*

* * *

Opening her eyes, she gazed dreamingly at it…at…at what held her love…as she stood alongside other women…looking at the ship…as it left the harbor. The crew had the fore, main, and mizzen course sails dropped. As they caught the breeze, the topsails were being lowered, and her love was gaining speed away from her. When would his voyage end and he return? Would he think of me on the cold, lonely nights? The topsails were in place, and with jibs unfurled, the power of the wind pushed the mighty ship to the south. A world away was its course. What a lonely life. When a man leaves, how does a woman survive, not knowing if her man will return? The north wind blew a cold air, and it cut into her. It was as if it wanted to chill her deep within her heart. Despite that, she didn't want to leave this place. She stood firm against the wind and watched her world disappear. She watched as the vessel carrying her life grew ever smaller against the sky, ever decreasing in size as the love for her man was increasing. Would he find a new love, perhaps, in some distant place? Would the scent of a new woman wipe his memory clear of her?

"Oh, did I tell him I love him?" I'm sure I did. Would it be enough to sustain him and bring him back? All she could do was wait. She could only wait as countless women have done over the ages. Staring into the bleakness, she saw nothing now. Nothing but a memory.

* * *

She turned and walked away.

Outside the terminal, Alex hailed a cab. She gave the driver Filemu's address. She needed to talk to a friend before she went back to her island, alone.

As the driver proceeded along the way to Filemu's house, Alex was deep in contemplation. It had only been days since she found Geoffrey washed up on her beach. A lifetime had been compressed into those days. It was hard for her to get her head around the totality of the events. One minute she had been alone on an island. The next thing she knew, she was in love, in love like she'd never been before. With Geoffrey, she found the true meaning of love. It was because of what this love caused in her that she truly came to know Iosefa and meet his incredible family. She only now realized the other love that had entered her life—the love of Jesus. She was still learning about this love. Grasping the deep underlying understanding of it all still eluded her. Filemu would help her find the answers to her many questions. She wanted to remove herself from the fear and doubt that had become part of her. *Why can I love but not trust? Why must I doubt?* These thoughts were on her mind. She was soon to find that evil seed sprouted can be uprooted and tossed aside. She only had to learn to recognize the tares from the wheat.

24

As the driver slowed and stopped, Alex realized she was at Filemu's house. A warm, secure feeling came over her. She felt a peace return to her heart. It was like she had come home after a long journey. The love inside would comfort her and ease the stress from the journey. She wanted to tell everything. She couldn't wait to get inside as she hurried up the walkway. Stopping at the door, she knocked. "Come in," she heard Filemu say.

She recognized the loving voice. It was saying welcome. It didn't matter who was knocking. It welcomed all into this house. It gave the love of the residents to everyone. That was the lesson she had learned from her teacher. Love is a gift, and one must share it.

Opening the door, Alex's first step inside transformed her. She felt as if she'd left only a minute ago. The feelings she felt on her first visit returned. The joy she had experienced listening to Iosefa on their boat ride was with her again. It was because evil could not enter this house. He knew he had to leave Alex when she entered. He'd wait. He is always waiting. He knows when the time is right to work against the light that he hates.

Alex walked over to Filemu. The dignified woman rose to greet her friend. With a loving hug, they kissed a cheek of the other. The two companions sat down. Even with her spirit uplifted, the strain of Geoffrey's leaving had left its mark on Alex's face. Filemu saw it. Even in the short time she had known Alex, she knew her well. She spoke.

"I'm so glad you came to visit me. My son didn't inform me you'd be here, so I assume you didn't tell him. I see you have a lot on your mind. I'm glad you thought of me as someone to talk to. Tell me what troubles you, my dear."

Her candor caught Alex somewhat off guard. She realized Filemu was a woman with great insight. Alex had it at one time. She had used it for the wrong purposes. Alex wanted to hear from someone smarter than herself. She wanted to learn. A person can only learn from someone with more discernment than themselves.

"Where do I start?" Alex stated. "I met a man, Filemu. We've only known each other for about a week. But it's been an incredible time. We fell in love. It seems strange that someone can fall in love in such a short time. I've thought I've loved before. I realized what I felt for him was different. No, it was just real. I found with him I'd never known true love until now. I know I loved before because I lost many loves in my life. I've felt I was being punished. I did terrible things to people. I did nothing illegal, but I hurt people and ruined lives with my greed. The losses all hurt me. That's why I came to my island. I wanted to escape losing loves. I didn't want to be punished anymore. Now he's left to take care of business. I fear he won't come back to me. I said terrible things to him. He's told me countless times that he loves me and he will be back. I cannot get this sense of doubt out of my mind. Am I being punished again? I want to trust him. I just can't seem to do it. I'm so confused. I don't know what to do." Tears were forming in her eyes as she sat back in her chair.

"Well, we have much to talk about. But I'll begin my remarks with something you must never forget. Everything is by the hand of God. He's at work in your life, Alex. You'll not find your answers from me. But I'll help you find them. But it's very important that you know God is a God of love. God is love. God cannot *punish* anyone. He may discipline you because he is your Father, and you are his child. Terrible things that happen to some people in this world are hard to understand. They are never an act of vengeance or punishment by God."

The woman continued. "Sit with your emotions. Feel them, listen to them, appreciate them, but never run from them. They will track you down and haunt you. You can only stop them when you are dauntless enough to face them. Then you'll learn the lessons they hold. If you aren't willing to learn, no one can help you. If you're determined to learn, no one can stop you.

"I've talked to you about Jesus and his light. Do not doubt in the darkness what God has shown you in the light. Doubts are messengers that God allows to be a part of our lives. They are the first knock at our door of things to be understood. Doubts will precede every uncertainty we first encounter when in a region unknown. Doubts are used by Satan against the light. Remember, God *allows* Satan to work in his world. You must know your enemy. The doubt he placed in Eve in the Garden of Eden precipitated the fall of man. God told Adam and Eve to "not eat from the tree of life or you will die." Satan then told Eve, "Surely, you will not die!" The doubt he spoke caused her to question God's word. A fatal mistake still today. There are things that must be done in faith, or they can never be. Faith is knowing God's will goes and does without our understanding. Not knowing, one can stand content in ignorance. Faith presses you into the hidden future by opening the path of action. The principal part of faith is patience. God's will does not have our sense of time.

"God expects us to walk in faith and trust. He allows us to be tested. There are many paths to go down in life. God creates one. Your mind creates the others. Be careful what you allow to enter your mind. God will show you the most wonderful things imaginable, providing you have the correct eyes to see them. The eyes are trust and faith. When the time is right, he'll allow your faith to be affirmed.

"I don't know this man of whom you speak. I cannot make a judgment about him. I can see that you love him. I'm glad you found someone to love. But remember this about love. Love someone, and your heart can be broken. That won't happen if you never give your love to anyone. Avoid all affection. You can wrap it up inside yourself. You can put it in a cold, dark place, and it will change. It will become unbreakable, insusceptible. To give love is to be vincible. You said the man you love left. I cannot comment on his returning.

"You mentioned about many loves lost. You have a new love now. This is a love you can never lose. Jesus loves you and will never leave you nor stop loving you. There's nothing you can do that will cause him to stop loving you. Never, ever. I know not what loves may come or go in your life, Alex. You may lose loves again. But you will never be without the one who loves you unconditionally—Jesus.

"Seek the answers you want in your faith and trust in God. He may reveal that what he desires for you differs from what you're working for. He doesn't want to deny your heart's desire. He wants what will truly make you happy. He wants to give you what will. Give yourself unconditionally to him and allow him to heal you. Acknowledge that he's in control and knows best. If you have faith and trust in God, he'll fulfill the most profound desires and dreams within you.

"God will speak to you when you don't expect it. He'll show you he's with you when you aren't looking. He'll be beside you when you think you are alone. This trust in him is what it's about, Alex. Once you have faith and trust in God, you will understand how to have faith and trust in others.

"May there be peace within you. May you trust that you are exactly where you are meant to be. May you not forget the infinite possibilities that are born of faith. May you pass on the love that has been given you. May you be content with yourself. Let this knowledge settle in your bones and allow your soul to sing, dance, and love. May you be safe, healthy, and happy. May you live in peace and bring light and joy to the world."

Alex looked at the woman and found another love. She knew it was another love she'd never lose. The love Filemu gave validated their friendship. Alex knew Filemu had given her love, and she wouldn't take that love back. Her love was the same as Jesus's. She'd entered this house thinking she was losing the only love she had. She now knew she was more loved than ever. With the love of Geoffrey in her heart, her heart blossomed like a rose on a sunny day in spring. A new sense of joy came over her. With it came a peace to her soul. The gift of unconditional love does that to a person. The power of this love created a new Alex once again. Ever learning, always growing in love's knowledge of Christ.

Alex suddenly realized all that she thought she knew she could pack in a small box. Its value was so paltry as to even be recognizable. The knowledge Filemu gave to her was of immeasurable wealth. And it was a gift. A gift. It had been heaven-sent. It had no comparison with anything previously valued by Alex. *Can people ever really lose anything when they possess the love of God?* she thought.

The two close friends sat and talked for hours. To Filemu, it was just another day serving God with love. To Alex, it was joy beyond any she ever felt, even with Geoffrey. She knew why. Anyone with a caring heart seeks the love between a woman and a man. Some find it. Some do not. She had found this love, the one she had searched for. It was greater than any of her dreams. Now she found another great love. The joy of it was that neither competed for more attention than the other. These loves are compatible because they come from a single source. We can trace all love to the fountainhead from which it flows. It begins with God.

Later, Alex retired to her hotel room. She and Filemu agreed to spend time together before she went back home. And there was no hurry. She was enjoying every minute with Filemu, Iosefa, and the rest of the family.

Her visit with Filemu ripped up the roots of the doubt planted. They dried and withered in the light that now shone on Alex. The sower of doubt knew he was losing this battle. Her faith had become stronger. He'd have to put a crack in her trust. He could use this weak spot to his advantage later. He is never deterred.

25

It was another typical day in the Western Caribbean when Geoffrey's Cayman Airlines flight landed on Grand Cayman Islands. He was glad his travels were concluded. For three days he had been hopping from one country to another. Money wasn't a problem, and neither were the few days. He had a second identity stored in Samoa with the first. He used this one to travel once he arrived in New Zealand. Geoffrey was a smart man and had considered every contingency. He knew he'd made it impossible for anyone to trace him here, even under an alias. He'd continue to use his new identity. His business dealings would be untraceable once his plan concluded. Getting his luggage, he went outside and took a taxi to his temporary home. After arriving in Chicago from Buenos Aires, using the hotel computer room, he'd rented a guest house in Georgetown on Grand Cayman for a month. It'd be a private place for him to stay and conduct his business. The key was where the real estate agent placed it. He went inside. It was perfect. This would be his office and home for the next two weeks. Tomorrow, he'd buy three computers and cell phones and the other equipment he'd need. What he wanted now was a shower and a nap.

After his rest, he called a cab and went to the main part of town. For tonight, he'd be a tourist. After spending time walking along the beach, he found a pleasant restaurant. He went in to the bar and ordered a glass of wine. He'd not felt this relaxed in quite some time.

There were people having fun. He noticed two women sitting further down the bar. The one sitting closest to him glanced his way. She looked at him and smiled. He smiled back. It was just like old times. A voice whispered in his head. *Go on down there and meet them. You deserve some companionship while you are here. What can it hurt?* He got up after smiling at the thought. Suddenly, something came from his heart. *No!* A sense of guilt came over him, and he sat back down.

It's just your first day here. There's no rush. Relax and enjoy dinner and go home. You've a lot of work for tomorrow, he reassured himself.

The next day, Geoffrey went to a car rental and rented a car. He then went to many locations to buy the equipment he needed. He didn't want to buy over one item at any location. It may draw attention to him. Once back at his villa, he connected his electronics. He set up a VPN, Tor, obfuscation tools, and anonymous emails to prevent anyone from tracing anything he did back to this house. He was ready to go to work. After completing online paperwork for dummy corporations, he was set. He'd start moving the funds around tomorrow. After a week to ten days, there'd be no trace to his Swiss bank account. He went to bed early. It had been a busy day. Although working while here, he felt like on a vacation. He wasn't looking over his shoulder for the first time in years. The anxiety had left him. He was secure. He had nothing to fear. At least that's what he thought.

After working most of the morning and into the afternoon, Geoffrey decided it was enough. *You're in a tropical resort. Enjoy yourself,* he kept hearing in his mind. He changed into his beachwear, grabbed a towel, and headed to a public beach. The fresh air felt good to him. He'd become accustomed to it. The sound of the surf was familiar. The crowds were not a problem for him. He rather enjoyed seeing the people. And why not? Here, everyone was having a grand time. He sat in the chair he'd brought with him. He realized his sense of peace was beyond anything he'd ever felt before. After all, Geoffrey Scott was dead. It felt like he had been reborn into a life of wealth and leisure. It was more than he'd dreamed when he first started his skimming from customers' accounts. The world was his oyster. A simple voice kept repeating itself. *You can do whatever you want.* It created a sense of power in his mind. Geoffrey was in complete control. It never felt as if someone was watching him. But evil was watching, waiting to catch Geoffrey in a weak moment. Evil is the best at watching and waiting.

After four days of work, Geoffrey's plans were coming together. All the pieces were in place. Money was moving. It was a game, and Geoffrey was having a glorious time playing this game. He knew the rules, and he knew how to play to win. That was how he played all his life, to win. Winning was what had been important. After the fourth day, he was feeling somewhat pompous. Money and power changes a person's perspective. Geoffrey was slowing drifting from the person he was. The one watching knew his time was right. It was time to turn Geoffrey toward his ways. Away from Alex.

Sensing his success, Geoffrey thought it was time to celebrate. He was ready for a night on the town. He readied himself for an evening of fun and drove to an area with many restaurants and night-spots. Walking into one, he went to the bar and ordered a glass of wine. He knew he'd never felt better in his life. He and the bartender engaged in the usual chitchat between two men in this situation. The bartender had just brought Geoffrey his second glass of wine when a server handed him a large order. "Enjoy your evening," he said to Geoffrey, as he turned to tend to business. The area was full of cheer-ful people. He smiled. *They'll go back to jobs they hate after they leave*, he thought with a smirk. *Not me.* With unseen help, Geoffrey was becoming a little full of himself. He glanced down the bar. He did a double take. It was the same woman he'd seen a few days ago at the other bar. She was alone at the moment. He couldn't believe it. Once again, something told him to go. He walked to where she sat.

"I know this sounds like a pickup line, but it's not. I swear I've seen you before. Have we met?" he said with an air of confidence.

"I don't think we have," she answered. "But I recognize your face. We were in the same bar a few days ago. I remember looking at you."

"Yes, that's where I saw you. I don't want to appear too forward, and I don't want to cause a scene by making a wrong assumption. Are you with anyone?"

"No, I'm alone. I work close by and stopped in here for a drink on the way home."

"I'm alone as well. My name is George Jackson. May I join you?"

"Please do. I'm Maggie Steward."

A sly grin came over the face of the one watching. *All in good time, all in good time*, he thought.

26

Alex arose from the dinner table with the other women to help Filemu with the dishes after dinner. They felt like she was part of the family. But that's the way it is with God's family. Sometimes it just takes time to meet new family members. Alex had never enjoyed days like she'd spent in this house with people she loved now. The time with Geoffrey was special. All loves are special. Loves that God bring into a life are so wonderful. There is no competition, only the joy of love itself. She knew it was time to return to her island. She had already discussed leaving tomorrow. Today was just another day in paradise. Alex sat in a chair and watched the family. It brought such a joy to her heart. She was a part of every conversation. Iakopo appeared tired as he said he was going to bed. He kissed everyone, including Alex, before he left the room. They were to go to their own rooms after he left. Slowly, everyone left except Filemu and Alex.

"Come sit beside me," the matriarch said to Alex.

"God has you in his care now. You must always trust in him. He loves you and wants the best for you. All he wants in return is for you to love him. Don't worry about tomorrow. Worry won't solve any problem. It will only take away today's joy. Do what you feel in your heart and trust God. He'll speak to you when he's ready. I look forward to a long friendship, Alex. Each day is the beginning of your life. Enjoy it. Each one is a gift."

"I love you, Filemu. You're the best friend any woman could have. I'll be back soon." Each gave a hug and kiss on the cheek. Alex left for the waiting cab to go to her hotel.

She woke early and prepared to leave. She stopped to pick up supplies before going to her boat. The eagerness to return to her island created a wonderful feeling. It brought her peace. She knew her future depended on her trust in God. She felt she had that trust. Boarding her boat, she left.

As Alex left the harbor, she headed west. She only passed a couple of fishing vessels. She did not focus her mind on her surroundings. She was repeating what Filemu told her. It had become such a beautiful story. She now knew what had caused her fear and anxiety. It was gone, never to return, or so she thought.

It was a simple course back to her island. She'd have no trouble getting there. She didn't realize her mind could process so many thoughts as it was doing now. Each floating around in her head like scraps of paper blown by a fan. She barely read one when another would float in front of her. She was approaching the northwest corner of Upolu when she heard the motor sputter and stop. The scraps of thoughts fell to the floor. Her heart sank with them.

She turned off the starter key and turned it back on. The engine cranked but didn't start. She had a problem. *Think, Alex. What did Iosefa tell you?* She looked at the fuel gauge. The tank was almost full. She opened the cover over the engine. Looking at the parts, she tried to remember what he had told her. After examining all the wiring, she concluded everything seemed to be attached. *God, what's going on? What's happened? What do I do?* Once again, she felt powerless while dealing with a problem. This time, the source of her solutions had stopped along with the engine. She sat down to think. She went over everything Iosefa told her about how this boat works. It was as if he had skipped this lesson. Deep inside of her, a sense of panic was growing. Her boat was adrift, and the trade wind would soon carry it away from the island into the vast, open Pacific Ocean. She drew on the lessons Filemu had taught her. The Bible verses were remembered. She went back to the helm and tried to start the engine. It never started. She knew she wouldn't be able to keep this up. Then there'd be no hope. *God, help me.*

She scanned the ocean toward Upolu to see if she could spot a boat. Now, there was none in sight. In a couple of hours, it'd be dark, and all hope would vanish. The chance was extreme that another vessel would be in the same spot as her tomorrow. The panic grew in her. She fought it. She knew who caused this in her before; she resolved herself not to let him in again. She couldn't stop thinking her journey of many years and many miles was to end in the middle of an endless ocean of water. All the wonders of life she had sought and then found would end.

I found faith I didn't even know existed until Iosefa talked to me about Jesus. I learned about it and trust. I think I understand. How can I prove it, Lord? What must I do? What must I say? Why all that trouble? Why all that effort? What was I supposed to learn that I missed, Lord? I ran away to this place. Then you brought Geoffrey into my life, and I found the love I'd always wanted. Now he's gone away. You opened my eyes to Iosefa and his family. I found you there, and I found joy. Now it's ending in days of despair with no land in sight? I know there's something else. I just know it. Please show me, Lord.

The faces of Filemu, Iosefa, and their family flashed before her eyes as tears formed in them. She could feel Geoffrey beside her, comforting her. She felt she was looking into his eyes at the kitchen table. All she could hear was him telling her how much he loved her. The tears were down her cheeks now. Then she heard a sound. She turned toward it.

Coming from out of nowhere was a small boat. A man was in it and headed toward her. The euphoria in her heart was immense. She waved her arms to be sure he saw her. Her excitement at the sight of a stranger was almost too much. She watched as his boat approached hers.

He pulled alongside. "I noticed your boat was sideways to the wind, and I didn't see any wake. I knew you were drifting. I thought I should come see if you needed any help."

"I was about to give up all hope. My engine stopped, and it won't start. This boat is new to me. I was told everything about operating it, but I can't understand what the problem is."

"Well, if I may come aboard, I'll look at it." He tossed her a line, and she tied his boat to hers. He climbed onto Alex's drifting platform.

"My name's Alex," she said.

"Hello," he answered. "I'll assume you're not just out of fuel."

"No, the tank is full."

"Go to the helm and turn the key. Let me see what's going on." She did as he instructed. The engine continued to crank but not start.

"Well, could be a couple of things. Do you have any tools?"

"Yes. My friend who helped me buy this boat gave me a toolbox with tools in it and a box of parts. He knows a lot about boats. He has a charter boat used for fishing. He told me he gave everything I may need. He's not told me what was in the toolbox or what the parts are for." Alex retrieved the boxes and gave them to the stranger.

Opening one, he took out a gauge with two wires attached. He removed a wire from a spark plug. "Turn on the ignition again," he said. She did as he wanted.

"You've got good spark. The problem lies elsewhere. The fuel lines are in good condition. I'll check the filter." Taking a wrench, he loosened the fuel line and removed the filter. Putting one end to his mouth, he blew into it. Nothing came out on the other end. Looking in the box of parts, he found another filter. He put the new filter in the fuel line and reconnected the parts. "Give the ignition a try now."

Alex turned the key, and the engine started. Her heart just about jumped out of her chest. "How can I ever thank you? I thought I was lost. It's a miracle you found me."

"It was just a simple clogged fuel filter. Lucky for you, your friend knows about boats. You don't go out on the Pacific Ocean without being able to deal with every contingency. You just have to solve problems. If you can't find the answer yourself, you need to seek help elsewhere."

"I spent my whole life doing just that, solving problems. Once again, when my life depended on it, I couldn't. I feel I owe you so much. I have nothing to offer."

"No problem," he said. "I suggest you proceed to where you were going. I'll be on my way now. Goodbye." He turned and climbed into his boat. He started his motor as she cast the line back to him.

They looked at each other. Alex was trying to understand what had just happened. It was too much. All that she'd learned from her time with Filemu welled up inside of her. She didn't know why she asked what she did. She just wanted to know.

"Do you know Jesus?"

The man in the boat looked back and smiled. "Very well," he said. He turned his boat and was away from hers. She watched him for a second and then realized she needed to sit. Shaking, she felt as she did on the mountain path after Geoffrey pulled her back. All those thoughts poured themselves out. Tears started rolling down her cheeks. She composed herself and stood to wave goodbye to another man who had saved her life. Looking in the direction that he'd left, she saw nothing. *I must have been sitting there longer than I thought. No*, she realized. *It had only been a few seconds. How did he get so far so fast?* she thought. She turned the boat to go to her island.

Alex grounded her boat on the soft sand of her beach. She was in a new world. It was a world without fear and anxiety. She had learned about love. True love. Many kinds of love. But most importantly, why love exists. Love exists as a gift from one that is love. Alex felt this love even though no one was around her. She'd learned that love exists in your heart, not in what is in your sight. The world trivialized the word *love* and didn't understand the true meaning of love. The world applied love to all things that were visually or physically pleasing, even if only temporal. At the moment, Alex felt more love than she thought possible. She knew why she was not adrift in the Pacific Ocean now. It was because God loved her unconditionally. She knew he loved her, and she'd never lose this love. Somehow, she knew God wanted more for her than to die abandoned in a vast expanse of water. She realized that this is the basis for trust. *I don't know what is to happen to me, Lord. But I know you want the best for me. Even when I think the worst, I know I can trust you for something better, something you have planned for me. I will always trust you and wait patiently for what you have planned for me.*

27

"Have you lived here long, Maggie?" her companion asked.

"About five years. I fell in love with the island on a vacation here. I lived and worked in New York City at that time. I had worked for the president of a large bank for many years. When I went back home, I started making inquiries about positions in the banking business here. There were many possibilities. With my resume, I could pick the job I wanted. The money was far below what I'd been making. The cost of living here is far below what I had been spending. I was fed up with the crowds and filth of the city. I hated the winters there. It was a simple decision to move. I have never regretted it. I assume you are a tourist."

"Yes, I guess it's easy for the locals to spot us. I thought I'd stay a couple of weeks to tend to my business here. I've worked hard for a few days and decided to be a full-time tourist. I'm out for a night on the town.

"We get many *tourists* like yourself," she said, emphasizing tourist. People come here to take care of business. I know the banking business on this island. I won't ask about your business here. I know you wouldn't tell me anyway. The work part of our lives is told. What were your plans here when you weren't working?"

"Your candor is refreshing. I enjoy a woman who gets to the point. To be honest, I've not thought about my free time here. But my free time is whenever I want it to be. I have no plans for this evening. Would you have dinner with me?"

"I was hoping you'd ask," she replied with a gleam in her eye.

He was feeling a sense of superiority never felt. Considering himself an average guy, he knew he had lived a good life, making good money. He wasn't that person anymore. Now he was in a class by itself. He was now in the top 10 percent, as some refer to the wealthy of the world. With that wealth came the ability to control his destiny. His ego was elevating his status of himself. He looked at the world-class beauty sitting across from him. The voice in his head spoke again. *It can only get better. Follow your desires.*

The server approached them. "Would you like another round?" she asked.

"Not at the moment. Please tell the maître d' we'd like to have dinner now. And I want a table in a quiet corner, please." He opened his billfold and took out a large denomination bill. "Give him this, please," he said as he handed her the bill. He smiled at her. She smiled back. She knew what he wanted. This was not her first day on the job. She nodded and left. The woman sitting across from him smiled. She enjoyed being with a man who was sure of himself. She knew this'd be a good evening. The new companions enjoyed light conversation while they waited for their table to be prepared. Each felt attracted to the other.

The server approached their table. Addressing the man, she said, "Your table is ready as you requested. Would you follow me, please?" She led them to a somewhat private dining area set apart from the general seating area.

"This will be fine," the man said to the server. He pulled a chair out for the woman and seated her. They each ordered another drink, and a wonderful dinner and conversation followed. At ease with each other, they enjoyed the evening.

After they concluded the meal, he asked her, "What do you locals do for entertainment in the evening?"

"We live in a tropical tourist resort town. There are many options. Do you enjoy listening to live music and dancing?"

"I love it," he answered. I can't remember the last time I did something like that. I know it will be special with you."

She smiled. "I have a favorite spot. It's where us locals hang out. We'll go whenever you're ready."

He motioned for the server. After paying his bill, they left.

"It's not far, and it's a beautiful night. Would you like to walk, or we can take a cab?"

"I'd love to walk along with you," he said. The two went on their way, hand in hand.

After they had walked a short way, she said, "Let's sit on that bench. I love to listen to the sound of the surf at night."

"That sounds good," he said. They sat side by side, enjoying the moment. *She's yours*, the voice in his head said. *You can have your wildest dreams now.*

His current situation was becoming his reality. *My past is just that*, he thought. *My past. Everything that had happened to me was to get me to this place. No one knows me. I have everything I could want. I may just stay here. Maybe with Maggie. Who knows what's coming for me?* he said to himself smugly. He was free, rich, and in a completely different world. What more could a man want?

Maggie turned and spoke to him. "I just love living on an island. Have you ever lived on an island?"

The words went into Geoffrey's ears with the power of a pair of clanging cymbals. It was as if he'd been on the most comfortable of beds, in the deepest of sleep, in the most wonderful of dreams. Suddenly, he didn't know where he was. He had a dazed look on his face. The face of Alex appeared in his mind. The voice in him spoke with dread. *At least you saw her. At least you knew her. It was a good a time. There will be more.*

Geoffrey shook his head. The actual reality was crystal clear now. He was going back to the same pointless life of self-indulgence, greed, and smugness. He was getting back on the same merry-go-round again. All he had now that he didn't have then was money. *Money. Is that all there is to life?* Remembering a moment on a mountain on the other side of the world, he knew there he'd found the truth to life he had sought. He didn't understand how that truth had been hidden from him since he came to the Cayman Islands. Life without Alex would be the same pointless life it had been before he washed up on her island. To stay here would be to never hold her in his arms, never to look into her eyes, never to feel her lips pressing against his again. He knew she was smarter than he. She found something that changed her. It had to have great value by the way it made her feel. She knew it made her better, and he wanted what she had. He wanted to know what she knew. *I always trusted your judgment then, Alex. I must trust it now. I'm coming back to you, Alex.*

A curse of anger was heard in the underworld. Geoffrey felt as if something went through him. He felt a sense of peace come over him. This feeling had eluded him since his arrival. His heart told him what to do. He'd do the right thing because he loved her. He wanted to be with his Alex again.

All the love he'd experienced on that island came flooding back into his memory. The evil that had been misdirecting him was gone. The snorkeling, the dinners, the moonlit walks, the beauty of her smile were as if they had happened only moments ago. Though thousands of miles away, she was beside him. He could smell the essence of her being. He could feel the touch of her hand on his. He knew what he had to do.

"Maggie, I don't know how to explain this. Actually, I can't. I've made a mistake. I made many mistakes in my life. I will not make any more. I've enjoyed our evening together, but I must leave now. I know you can find your way home. I wish you well." Geoffrey rose and walked away.

Maggie looked at Geoffrey's back as he walked away. With a look of disgust on her face, she said to herself, *Well, Maggie, you did it again. You sure can pick the losers. Well, at least I got a wonderful dinner out of it.* She sat looking at the dark night sky, reflecting on the island she was on.

28

❧

Upon arriving back at his bungalow, Geoffrey hurried inside. He poured a glass of wine and went to sit on his patio. A gentle breeze was blowing. The surf flowing onshore was a familiar sound. It felt as if Alex was sitting beside him. After an hour, he went to bed. It'd be the most restful sleep of his time here.

Geoffrey awoke the next morning and arose a new man—the man he felt he'd longed to be. He had two things he'd never had. All he needed were these. His money would be there, but his life was more important. He had a love and purpose for that love. He somehow felt this was what he had sought. Preparing a pot of coffee, he went to work. Only one thing was on his mind, to complete his work and return to where he belonged, by his Alex. He'd be on the flight he told her he'd be on. He'd not disappoint her. *I can never disappoint her,* he said to himself. *She always deserves better.*

Geoffrey had always been seeking his future. He never knew what that future was. It's been said the best way to know the future is to write it yourself. Said another way, the best way to know what you should do is to do what you would do. In love, Geoffrey knew what he'd do. He'd finish his work and move on. The direction of an anchored ship is impossible to change. He knew if he stayed here, anchored in his past, he'd have eventually rusted away. The direction of a moving ship is easy to change. He was moving and on a timetable. He'd complete his transactions. There were a few more matters to attend to. He'd do it for Alex. He would do it because he loved her. Then he'd be on the plane he told Alex he'd be on. He would for a lot of reasons. One of them was because he knew she'd be there waiting for him.

His days seemed to drag on. The plans were being completed. A fortune would soon be secure. He wished he could speed the earth on its rotation. He didn't know if he could wait to hold her in his arms again. But the time passed.

He boarded an Air Canada flight to Montreal. From there he'd fly to San Francisco, then to Honolulu, then to Samoa. Just another Canadian visiting an island. There, he'd fall in love with this island and stay. His new life would be the rest. His anticipation was almost beyond his ability to control.

* * *

Alex was waiting for the dawn to arrive. It was the twenty-first day since Geoffrey had left. It was the day he said he'd be returning. She went outside on her porch with her morning coffee. Looking out over her world, she was at peace. She was always at peace now. She had put her trust in God and knew, no matter what happened, he wouldn't disappoint her. He wanted the best for her, and what he gave she knew would be just that. Each day was now to enjoy. She went back inside and dressed to leave. She boarded her boat and proceeded to Apia. Upon arriving at the harbor, she docked and took a cab to the airport. Once there, she checked the incoming schedules. She saw the Fiji Airways flight from San Francisco would arrive in a few hours. She went to a seating area where she could watch the incoming airplanes. As anxiety would come over her, she'd put it aside. She had a helper now that took her troubles away. But deep inside of her, she knew what she wanted. She was human and a woman. A woman in love. *Please, God, if it be your will, bring him back to me.* For the next couple of hours, she watched the planes land one by one. The same scene was repeated after each landing as people left the plane. Joyous people reunited with loved ones, walking down the concourse toward their lives. Oh, how she wanted to join them.

The time arrived for the flight she'd been expecting to land. She looked at the sky to the east. She saw a plane descending. As it approached the runway, she saw the logo of Fiji Airways on the plane. Her heart raced. She watched as it touched down and taxied to the gate. Her heart was now pounding. She was shaking. *I'm sorry, God. You know how much I want to see him. Whether or not he's on the plane, I will still love you and trust you.* She strolled toward the waiting area just outside the customs exit. She sat down.

As people left the plane, they crowded into the customs area. The crowd slowly made their way through and into the arms of family and friends waiting for them. Alex peered into the faces as they came into her view. She recognized none. The crowd thinned and the people entering customs became fewer. It appeared that no one else was to leave the plane. Her heart paused as she sensed the possibility that maybe she could not have the doll she wanted. That maybe… maybe…maybe…her being could not contain her excitement. *There. There he is. He's rounding the corner. Is it really him? Yes. Yes! It is him! It's Geoffrey! He's come back! He's come back to me!* Tears of such joy were flowing down her face. She'd forgotten how to rise and walk. *Oh, Geoffrey, you came back! You came back like you said you would! You told me you would! I wish so that I'd believed you then! Thank you, God! Oh, God, thank you!* She sprang to her feet. She ran to the area just a foot past where he'd walk to her. He walked past the checkpoint, dropped his bags, and grabbed her. Lifting her off the ground, he twirled her around and around and around and around, in a never-ending embrace and kiss. He held her feet off the floor. It didn't matter. She wouldn't have felt her feet on the ground if he wasn't holding her. She was in a dream. A real dream. A dream that was reality. A dream come true. In a life, love and trust can create such events.

They went home.

Sitting on the porch together, they felt as couples have felt for millennia. No one can express this feeling with words. This feeling must be experienced. It's because each experience is unique. The Creator begets it uniquely for just that couple. This couple experienced what he planned for them.

"Alex, I completed my plans while I was in the Cayman Islands. My money is safe and available. It's untraceable, as am I. I want to give you a token of my love. You not only saved my life, but you gave me a new life. A life better than I could have dreamed. So to show you my love, I relinquish all else. After transferring my money to a safe Swiss numbered account, I contacted an attorney. He made a power of attorney. It appoints you with power over my assets. The money belongs to you. I give it not because you need it or want it. I give it to you so you know there's no greater love in me than my love for you. I know you will use the funds for a better good than I. All I care about now is you. I trust you. I love you, Alex."

Could her heart contain her joy? No, it was beyond that. The moment was beyond any of their wildest imaginations. But it seemed real. She felt it. She was living it. She wondered. Was her life a dream? Or was a dream her life?

29

❦

The princess awoke. Light pouring in through the window opening of the castle sparkled and twinkled in a never-ending stream. The dust particles in the air turned golden by the luminance of the sun's gift this day. The blue color of her eyes appeared as deep as the sky that held this morning's dawn. Its hue was more vivid than the blue birds sitting on her windowsill. He had carefully written their morning song for only her, and they sang it with passion. Her eyes were as bright as any light. If the joy in her heart could speak, it'd have waxed eloquent with words unequalled by the greatest of poets. She rose and walked across the room as if she had no weight. Into the mirror went her gaze, and what looked back was beyond any of her dreams. What she viewed filled her with something she had rarely seen or felt and seldom given in her life long ago. Love had caused this beauty and effervescence of her soul, and it shone all around her. She looked at the creatures watching her and smiled.

She wasn't sure why these thoughts were in her. She didn't feel as if she had put on a glass slipper nor like she had let down her long hair. No dragon had been slain. She had countered no witch's poison. The wonderings of her mind wouldn't find the answer this time. They never had. But something *magical* had happened.

God's love had won the battle. Long ago, Alex had wondered what the secret was. What was the mystery? Now she knew. All the questions of her life were solved with two words, *God's love*. When it's possessed, all evil vanishes. It seems enchanting, *magical*. It's a gift. One only has to take and accept it whence it's given.

Alex was preparing to move on. She was bundling all her past in a box to be put away. In it, she packed something that she had never understood. But she understood now; she'd never need nor use them again. The illusions she had lived with were now part of her past. All of her past she put in this box. She'd place it in the attic of her mind with all the other relics of her past life. The door wouldn't open again after it was closed. She now knew the truth. With God, there is no past. There is no use for such to ponder. There is only today. Today is the gift. She would live it fully, in love with all.

Alex had changed. She'd once been in control. She now relinquished this control over to God. Her commanding nature had been replaced with a humility that shone the joy in her heart. She had also changed that which was within her mind. She now recognized the difference between unrealistic illusions and hope eternal. She knew where to place her faith and trust. She placed it where she was first loved.

* * *

But everyone should always flavor life with a little of the spice of fantasy. We should never stop dreaming. That is also a gift. It's a glimpse into the potential by the Creator. He allows us to dream what is possible. We must always trust in him. He wants the best for us, and with him, all things *are* possible. With dreams and faith, one never knows what he may cause to *wash up on their beach*.

* * *

Entering the room, Geoffrey walked to Alex. Putting his hands on her shoulders, he looked at her reflection in the mirror. Their eyes spoke of the special love that was given to a man and woman to share. "Let's go start a life together," she said.

"I'm with you, always," her love answered.

The End

ABOUT THE AUTHOR

Raised by Christian parents in Beaumont, Texas, the author recalls his boyhood fondly. Those memories of his youth left an indelible mark on his heart. But many tragedies lay ahead. His faith in Jesus Christ would give him strength as his Christian faith matured.

After thirty years of marriage, his first wife died from cancer. Their three children had all recently married and were starting families of their own.

Though married for fifty years, he was to experience the loss of two more wives—one more to cancer and the last to stroke. Questions of faith were not easily or quickly answered. The company and counsel of his pastors, friends, and church family, time spent in prayer, and Bible study have sustained him.

He previously published his first novel, *Sarah*. He writes the weekly prayer for his church printed in the Sunday bulletin and posted on the church website. He enjoys writing and is working on two more novels.

Tommy Raykovich lives at Hilltop Lakes, Texas. He's a member of Hilltop Lakes Chapel and serves on the board of trustees at the church, enjoying volunteer work in many church functions.

He also serves on the Board of Directors of Hospice Brazos Valley.

9 798886 857092